A Debate
on Jewish Emancipation
and Christian Theology
in Old Berlin

A Debate
on Jewish Emancipation
and Christian Theology
in Old Berlin

David Friedländer,
Friedrich Schleiermacher,
Wilhelm Abraham Teller

Edited and translated by
Richard Crouter and Julie Klassen

Hackett Publishing Company, Inc.
Indianapolis/Cambridge

Printed in the United States of America

10 09 08 07 06 05 04   1 2 3 4 5 6 7

For further information, please address
Hackett Publishing Company, Inc.
P. O. Box 44937
Indianapolis, Indiana 46244–0937

www.hackettpublishing.com

Cover design by Listenberger Design & Associates and Jennifer Plumley
Text design by Chris Downey
Composition by William Hartman
Printed at Sheridan Books, Inc.

Library of Congress Cataloging-in-Publication Data

A debate on Jewish emancipation and Christian theology in old Berlin / David
   Friedländer, Friedrich Schleiermacher, Wilhelm Abraham Teller ; edited and
   translated by Richard Crouter and Julie Klassen.
       p. cm.
       Includes English translation of Politisch-theologische Aufgabe über die
   Behandlung der jüdischen Täuflinge.
       Includes bibliographical references and index.
       ISBN 0-87220-720-X (cloth : alk. paper) — ISBN 0-87220-719-6
   (pbk. : alk. paper)
       1. Jews—Emancipation—Germany—Prussia. 2. Jews—Legal status,
   laws, etc.—Germany—Prussia. 3. Jews—Conversion to Christianity—
   Germany—Prussia. 4. Jews—Civil rights—Germany—Prussia. 5. Prussia
   (Germany)—Religion—18th century. 6. Berlin (Germany)—Ethnic relations.
   I. Friedländer, David, 1750–1834. Sendschreiben an seine Hochwürden Herrn
   Oberconsistorialrath und Probst Teller zu Berlin, von einigen Hausvätern
   Jüdischer Religion. English. II. Schleiermacher, Friedrich, 1768–1834. Briefe
   bei Gelegenheit der politisch theologischen Aufgabe und des Sendschreibens
   jüdischer Hausväter. English. III. Teller, Wilhelm Abraham, 1734–1804.
   Beantwortung des Sendschreibens einiger Hausväter jüdischer Religion an
   mich den Probst Teller. English. IV. Crouter, Richard. V. Klassen, Julie A.
   VI. Politisch-theologische Aufgabe über die Behandlung der jüdischen
   Täuflinge. English.

   DS135.G34D44 2004
   261.2'6'0943—dc22

The paper used in this publication meets the minimum requirements of American National Standard for Information Sciences—Permanence of Paper for
Printed Library Materials, ANSI Z39.48–1984.

∞

Contents

Acknowledgments

A number of colleagues and institutions have encouraged and assisted us in developing and bringing this project to completion. We are grateful to Michael A. Meyer, Hebrew Union College, for reviewing an early prospectus and suggesting that we include Wilhelm Abraham Teller's response in the collection of translated texts. Günter Meckenstock, Christian-Albrechts-Universität, Kiel, Germany, graciously provided resources from the Schleiermacher-Forschungsstelle, where the relevant volume of the Friedrich Schleiermacher critical edition (*KGA* I.2) was produced for Walter de Gruyter. Colleagues within the German Studies Association, especially Leslie A. Adelson, Susannah Heschel, Jonathan M. Hess, Hillel J. Kieval, and Steven Lowenstein, offered encouragement and shared their own scholarly interest in this significant debate between German Jewry and Protestant theology, as did colleagues within the Nineteenth-Century Theology Group of the American Academy of Religion, especially Ted Vial and Walter Wyman, Jr.

We are grateful to these persons as well as to other colleagues and friends who share our sense of poignancy with regard to relations between Christians and Jews in German history.

Chronology

1729	Moses Mendelssohn is born in Dessau; Gotthold Ephraim Lessing is born in Kamenz.
1734	Wilhelm Abraham Teller is born in Leipzig.
1740–86	Friedrich II (the Great) is king of Prussia.
1742	Mendelssohn is in Berlin as a bookkeeper and as a philosopher within the Jewish *Haskalah.*
1750	David Friedländer is born in Königsberg to the silk merchant Joachim Moses Friedländer.
1756–63	Seven Years' War.
1762	Rousseau publishes *Emile* and *The Social Contract.*
1767–1804	Popular Enlightenment theologian Wilhelm Abraham Teller serves as provost and supreme consistorial counselor of the Protestant Church in Berlin.
1768	Schleiermacher is born in Breslau in Lower Silesia to a family steeped in Moravian (Herrnhuter) Pietism.
1771–1834	Friedländer is active in Berlin as an industrialist and Jewish community leader
1778	Friedländer joins Mendelssohn in founding the Jewish Free School in Berlin.
1779	Lessing publishes *Nathan the Wise,* modeled on Mendelssohn.
1781	Lessing dies; Wilhelm von Dohm publishes *On the Civil Improvement of the Jews;* Kant publishes *The Critique of Pure Reason.*
1782	Herder publishes *The Spirit of Hebrew Poetry;* Joseph II enacts the Edict of Toleration for the Jews of Vienna and Lower Austria.
1783	Mendelssohn publishes *Jerusalem, or on Religious Power and Judaism.*

1783–5	Schleiermacher attends Moravian boarding schools.
1786	Moses Mendelssohn dies; Friedländer emerges as the heir of Mendelssohn.
1786–97	Friedrich Wilhelm II, king of Prussia, ushers in an era of Jewish aspiration.
1787	Storming of the Bastille.
1787–90	Schleiermacher attends the University of Halle.
1787–92	Friedländer, as a general deputy of Prussian Jewry, works for Jewish rights in Prussia.
1788	Friedländer publishes *Open Letter to the German Jews.*
1791	Friedländer is granted German citizenship without hereditary rights for his children.
1793	King Louis XVI of France is executed; Kant publishes *Religion within the Limits of Reason Alone.*
1793	Friedländer publishes *Documentary Collection concerning the Reform of the Jewish Colonies in Prussia.*
1796–1802	Schleiermacher is active in the Romantic circle in Berlin with the brothers A. W. and Friedrich Schlegel, Dorothea Veit, and Henriette Herz.
1797–1840	Friedrich Wilhelm III is king of Prussia.
1797	The Hebrew language version of the *Haskalah* journal *Ha-meassef* ("The Collector") ceases publication.
1797	Schleiermacher becomes a Protestant chaplain at the Charité, a hospital in Berlin.
1798–1800	The three-volume *Athenaeum,* the literary organ of the Berlin Romantics, is published.
1799	[March] *Political-Theological Task concerning the Treatment of Baptized Jews* is published anonymously.
1799	[April] Friedländer publishes *Open Letter to Provost Teller* anonymously.
1799	[June] Schleiermacher publishes *On Religion: Speeches to Its Cultured Despisers* anonymously.

1799	[July] Schleiermacher publishes *Letters on the Occasion of the Political-Theological Task and the Open Letter of Jewish Householders* anonymously.
1799	Teller publishes *Response to the Open Letter*
1804	Teller dies; Friedländer retires from business to devote himself exclusively to public service.
1809–34	Schleiermacher is a professor of theology at the University of Berlin and a member of the Berlin Academy of Sciences.
1810–34	Schleiermacher is a preacher at Holy Trinity Church in Berlin.
1811	[January 11] Friedländer petitions the government in opposition to Jewish baptisms.
1812	The Prussian reform government (Stein, Hardenberg) issues the Edict of Emancipation for Jews.
1815	The Congress of Vienna settles the Napoleonic wars, reshapes European politics, and ushers in an era of reaction on the "Jewish question."
1818–32	Hegel teaches at the University of Berlin.
1821–2	Schleiermacher publishes the first edition of his systematic theology, *The Christian Faith [Glaubenslehre]*.
1831	Hegel dies.
1832	Goethe dies.
1834	Schleiermacher and Friedländer die.
1869	[July 3] The Reichstag of the Northern German Confederation grants Jews civil and political rights without a religious test.
1913	The Imperial Citizenship Law (*Reichs und Staatsangehörigkeitsgesetz*) grants citizenship to German Jews and retains heredity as the basis for citizenship.

A Note On Translations

Throughout this work our aim as translators is to provide reliable and coherent English versions of these original German documents. We have sought to combine fidelity to the original with a level of English that is comprehensible to today's readers. If the texts occasionally have an old-fashioned ring, that quality serves as a reminder that they originated in a different period of history. All of the present texts are freshly translated in their entirety from the German and placed in a readable, annotated edition. When a footnote is preceded by "[Eds.]", an explanatory or reference note has been added. Otherwise, reference or other material in footnotes belongs to the original German writers.

The relatively short and satirical anonymously published *"Political-Theological Task"* is presented in English translation for the first time here. Although it is believed to derive from the circle around Friedländer, this tract from March 1799 appeared anonymously as "Politisch-theologische Aufgabe über die Behandlung der jüdischen Täuflinge," *Berlinisches Archiv der Zeit und ihres Geschmacks* 5 (Berlin, 1799), Teilbd. 1: 228–39, and is translated from Günter Meckenstock, ed., Friedrich Schleiermacher, *Kritische Gesamtausgabe I Schriften und Entwürfe. Band 2 Schriften aus der Berliner Zeit 1796–1799* (Berlin: Walter de Gruyter, 1984) 373–80. The same volume of the new critical edition of Schleiermacher has been used for the German original of Friedländer's *Open Letter* (KGA I.2: 381–413) as well as for Schleiermacher's *Letters on the Occasion* (KGA I.2: 327–61). Of these two texts, excerpts of Friedländer's plea for baptism as a vehicle for gaining entrance to civil society previously appeared in Paul Mendes-Flohr and Jehuda Reinharz, eds., *The Jew in the Modern World: A Documentary History*, 2nd edition (New York: Oxford, 1995) 105–11. More recently, Gilya G. Schmidt published a translation of the six Schleiermacher letters with the Edwin Mellen Press (2001). This hardbound edition does not provide the surrounding documents of the debate to which Schleiermacher refers. Translation of Teller's *Response* is based upon the original German 2nd edition of *Beantwortung des Sendschreibens einiger Hausväter jüdischer Religion an mich den Probst Teller* (Berlin: August Mylius, 1799).

A comment is in order about gender-linked wording. We have adhered to the German texts' masculine terminology in our translation of third person singular abstract pronouns as "he," "him," and "his," as well as masculine collective concepts, such as "mankind." The use of gender-neutral terms for the English version would be inauthentic for its time and also misrepresent the authors' arguments, since the civil rights under discussion were available only to men, with ancillary benefits for wives and dependents derived only through the heads of households.

Further Reading

Aleinikoff, T. Alexander and Douglas Klusmeyer, eds. *Citizenship Today: Global Perspectives and Practices.* Washington, DC: Brookings Institution Press, 2001.

———. *From Migrants to Citizens: Membership in a Changing World.* Washington, DC: Brookings Institution Press, 2000.

Bade, Klaus J. "Immigration, Naturalization, and Ethno-National Traditions in Germany: From the Citizenship Law of 1913 to the Law of 1999." In *Crossing Boundaries: The Exclusion and Inclusion of Minorities in Germany and Austria,* edited by Larry Eugene Jones. New York: Berghahn Books, 2001.

Brenner, Michael. *Emancipation and Acculturation 1780–1871,* vol. 2 of *German-Jewish History in Modern Times,* edited by Michael A. Meyer. New York: Columbia University Press, 1997.

Crouter, Richard, ed. and tr. Introduction to *On Religion: Speeches to Its Cultured Despisers,* by Friedrich Schleiermacher. Cambridge: Cambridge University Press, 1996.

Hess, Jonathan. *Germans, Jews, and the Claims of Modernity.* New Haven: Yale University Press, 2002.

Katz, Jacob. *Out of the Ghetto: The Social Background of Jewish Emancipation 1770–1870.* New York: Schocken Books, 1973.

Lowenstein, Steven M. *The Jewishness of David Friedländer and the Crisis of Berlin Jewry.* Ramat-Gan, Israel: Bar-Ilan University, 1994.

Meyer, Michael A. *The Origins of the Modern Jew: Jewish Identity and European Culture in Germany, 1749–1824.* Detroit: Wayne State University Press, 1979.

Nachama, Andreas, Julius H. Schoeps, and Hermann Simon. *Jews in Berlin.* New York: Berghahn, 2003.

Şenocak, Zafer. *Atlas of a Tropical Germany: Essays on Politics and Culture, 1990–1998.* Translated and edited by Leslie A. Adelson. Lincoln, NE: University of Nebraska Press, 2000.

Introduction

Jewish Aspirations in Protestant Prussia

The story set forth in this poignant collection of Jewish and Christian texts is age-old, yet its permutations are widely present in today's world.[1] At one level, this is the story of a typical clash between Enlightenment universal human rights and traditional religious values. As Moses Mendelssohn's 1783 masterpiece, *Jerusalem, or on Religious Power and Judaism,* makes clear, the rising aspirations of German Jews are embedded in a tangled history of relations between church and state. In Mendelssohn's day, and in ours, that history includes a series of partial settlements and political compromises that illustrate the perennial problems of religion, ethnicity, and citizenship. Although the texts that follow best convey their own meaning, a word on this critical period in Prussia's Jewish-Christian relations will set the stage for a reading of these texts.

Brought together in an English edition for the first time, each source was originally published between March and summer of 1799 as an article or pamphlet-sized book. Except for the work of Wilhelm Abraham Teller, all first appeared anonymously. Together the texts enable readers to sense firsthand the aspirations of Jews who sought to live out the legacy of Mendelssohn ("of blessed memory," in Teller's words) by seeking to negotiate civil liberties and religious freedom with the Prussian government. The youngest representative in this volume, Friedrich Schleiermacher, is today the figure who is best known, having subsequently risen to prominence as the founder of modern Protestant thought. At the time, however, the repute and social standing of David Friedländer, wealthy industrialist and Jewish community leader, and his addressee, Wilhelm Abraham Teller, provost and head of the Protestant Church in Berlin, far exceeded that of the 30-year-old preacher. Both figures had enjoyed years of success within the political and commercial development of a rapidly growing Berlin. Younger than Teller by sixteen years, Friedländer also stood at the height of his influence. Neither

---

1. See the Postscript to this volume.

figure engaged in the sharply polemical satire of the Schleiermacher *Letters* or the Jewish *Political-Theological Task,* whose unknown author launched this debate in March 1799. Along with Friedländer's *Open Letter* and Teller's *Response,* these texts provide an all-too-rare instance of enlightened Jewish and Protestant men of affairs who argue with passion and reason for a principled solution to the issues at hand.[2] The tormented history of Christian theological responses to Jewish aspiration shows all-too-few such examples of literate civility in religious and political discussions. It is hoped that, in addition to appreciating the specific dilemmas and issues raised by the debate, students of these texts will recognize the perennial relevance of eighteenth-century ideals of universal human dignity and equality in the struggle for political and religious freedom, or even for sheer survival.[3]

Of course, an especially biting quality clings to this narrative. Since the dramatic exchange arose within the most powerful state in Germany, we cannot think about it today apart from awareness of how the nineteenth-century denial of Jewish civil life became totalized and transformed into virulent anti-Semitism and eventually into the eliminationist policies of the Hitler regime. Yet those distant events were wholly unforeseen by the progressive and liberal minds of Friedländer, Schleiermacher, and Teller as these protagonists discussed the political fate of Berlin's and Prussia's Jews.

Setting the Stage

In the late eighteenth century the masses of German Jews remained largely a separate and distinct culture. These Ashkenazi (Central

2. This debate over the plight of religious confessions within a European city is reminiscent of the sixteenth-century debate over Geneva between John Calvin and his Catholic counterpart Jacopo Sadoleto. See John Calvin and Jacopo Sadoleto, *A Reformation Debate: Sadoleto's Letter to the Genevans and Calvin's Reply,* ed. John C. Olin (Grand Rapids, MI: Baker Book House, 1979). In both instances we encounter a sharp but civil religious controversy that has real-world consequences for a specific historical time and place.

3. As contemporary examples one need look no further than the plight of Kurds in Turkey, the Tibetans in China, the Papuans in Indonesia, or the Burakumin in Japan. Indeed, David Maybury-Lewis notes that 5 percent of the world's population of indigenous peoples is involved in a struggle for cultural survival. See his *Indigenous Peoples, Ethnic Groups, and the State* (Boston: Allyn and Bacon, 1997).

European) Jews were generally poor, were uneducated in the larger German culture while retaining their age-old traditions, and spoke a form of Judeo-German that we have come to call Yiddish. Even though the stirrings of human rights in Germany of the 1780s and 1790s were real and tangible, it was, in the words of Werner G. Mosse, "a long bumpy road to emancipation."[4] The philosopher king, Friedrich the Great, had brought the European Enlightenment to his court at Potsdam. But his decidedly negative views of Jews did not auger well for the future. Even so, responding to the request of Moses Mendelssohn, the king's civil servant, Christian Wilhelm von Dohm, wrote a major plea, *On the Civil Improvement of the Jews*, in 1781.[5] Within a few years other better-known revolutionary works appeared in Germany and in America. Immanuel Kant published *The Critique of Pure Reason* that same year, while Thomas Jefferson's *Notes on the State of Virginia*, which directly addressed the issue of church and state, appeared in 1782. When French Jews were granted equality in 1791 as a result of the revolution, those events set off significant repercussions in German lands, which found themselves fearful of Jacobinic radicalism and lacked a uniform policy or an orderly legal means of improving the Jews' legal status.[6] Upon Friedrich the Great's death in 1786, his son Friedrich Wilhelm II (1786–97) ushered in a period of hope as well as an official policy of religious repression. When Friedrich Wilhelm III (1797–1840) came to power, self-styled liberal and enlightened Christian writers again sought to come to terms with the thwarted aspirations of Berlin's Jewish elite. Yet this exercise in the rhetoric of religious and political policymaking was some years ahead of the ability of the German situation to enact the desired reforms. In keeping

4. Werner G. Mosse, "From 'Schutzjuden' to 'Deutsche Staatsbürger Jüdischen Glaubens': The Long and Bumpy Road of Jewish Emancipation in Germany," in *Paths of Emancipation: Jews, States, and Citizenship*, eds. Pierre and Ira Katznelson Birnbaum (Princeton: Princeton University Press, 1995).

5. The German original is book length. Selections from the Dohm treatise are found in Paul Mendes-Flohr and Jehuda Reinharz, eds., *The Jew in the Modern World: A Documentary History*, 2nd edition (New York: Oxford University Press, 1995), 28–36.

6. Michael Brenner, *Emancipation and Acculturation 1780–1871*, vol. 2 of *German-Jewish History in Modern Times*, ed. Michael A. Meyer (New York: Columbia University Press, 1997), 19.

with the new relative social mobility accorded to upper class Jews, the temptations to pursue more radical forms of assimilation and to convert to Christianity increased dramatically.[7]

The 1799 discussion of legal equality of Jews and Christians produced no immediate results. To be sure, progress was achieved during the era of Prussian reform (1809–12), which issued a decree of emancipation for Berlin's Jews in March 1812. But this measure soon fell victim to a politics of conservative restoration in the aftermath of the Napoleonic wars and the 1815 Congress of Vienna. Christian and European anti-Semitic stereotypes impeded progress at every step. Official civil and political rights for German Jews were achieved only after another seventy years. In contrast with the Enlightenment ideals of France and America, the German sense of nationhood was based on blood ties more than on a philosophical argument for human rights. On July 3, 1869, the Reichstag of the Northern German Confederation finally passed a law that declared, "All still existent restrictions on civil and political rights derived from the difference in religious confession are hereby repealed."[8] But rights guaranteed in law were, even then, not to be permanent. The aftermath of the 1913 Imperial Citizenship Law, which again granted citizenship to German Jews, is sketched in the Postscript to this volume.

Prominent silk merchant, friend of the nobility, intellectual and spiritual heir of Moses Mendelssohn, proponent of *Haskalah* (Jewish Enlightenment) within the Berlin community, David Friedländer (1750–1834) felt the full weight of his social prominence and religious leadership by the late 1790s. If Mendelssohn's reputation has vacillated and suffered in recent years, owing to a post-Holocaust suspicion of German Jewish acculturation, this is even more the case with Friedländer. Social class, aspirations of Enlightenment Jews (*Maskilim*) for their community, and shifting tides of politics all conspired to shape his long career. Historian of modern Judaism Michael A. Meyer characterizes Friedländer as having the dilemma of how best to perpetuate

---

7. Steven M. Lowenstein, *The Jewishness of David Friedländer and the Crisis of Berlin Jewry* (Ramat-Gan, Israel: Bar-Ilan University, 1994), 27–30, treats this "baptism epidemic," which included the children of Moses Mendelssohn and his noted grandson, the composer Felix Mendelssohn.

8. Cited in Mendes-Flohr and Reinharz, *The Jew in the Modern World*, 153.

the meaning of his master while pressing further the matter of political rights for Berlin Jews.[9] Friedländer had known Mendelssohn intimately and continuously since coming to Berlin in 1771. In 1778 he joined Mendelssohn in establishing the Jewish Free School in Berlin; he soon became a director of the school as well as the director of a Hebrew publishing house. In these capacities Friedländer produced a German reader with the aim of broadening and modernizing Jewish education. Since there was no obvious heir to Mendelssohn, circumstances and his own ambition thrust Friedländer into this role. Owing to his longevity—he died in 1834, the same year as Schleiermacher—Friedländer experienced several cycles of hope and disappointment in Jewish-German relations.

Following Mendelssohn's death, Friedländer's role was fraught with ambiguity. He repeatedly sought to inculcate Jewish and Enlightenment values by publishing articles in the *Berlinische Monatsschrift* and by translating the traditional prayer book and other Hebrew material into German. Meyer notes that Friedländer moved beyond Mendelssohn in two ways: "He denied the claim of a revealed ceremonial law, which had been maintained by Mendelssohn; and he strove to extend Jewish cultural emancipation into the political sphere."[10] Born to great wealth that was further enhanced by marriage into the Berlin family of Daniel Itzig,[11] Friedländer's elitism held popular religious practices in disdain. In 1790 he wrote in the *Berlinische Monatsschrift:* "The great mass of the Jews is characterized by a babbling away of their prayers, conscientious observance of religious ceremonies, and other outward piety, just like the riffraff of other religious groups."[12]

Yet, as Steven M. Lowenstein shows, Friedländer never lost an emotional attachment to his Jewishness and to the causes of

---

9. Michael A. Meyer, *The Origins of the Modern Jew: Jewish Identity and European Culture in Germany, 1749–1824* (Detroit: Wayne State University Press, 1979), 57–84.

10. Meyer, *Origins,* 59.

11. Steven M. Lowenstein, "Jewish Upper Crust and Berlin Jewish Enlightenment: The Family of Daniel Itzig," in *From East to West: Jews in a Changing Europe 1750–1870,* ed. Frances Malino and David Sorkin (Oxford: Basil Blackwell, 1990), 182–201.

12. Cited in Meyer, *Origins,* 61.

Judaism, even as he brought his significant influence to bear on
its reform. Although a radical champion of Enlightenment,
Friedländer criticized the efforts of the Jewish elite to attain separate status from the Jewish masses in Prussia. When members
of his own family refused to pay their annual dues to the Jewish
community, Friedländer paid on their behalf.[13] Despite his harsh
criticism of the popular religion of the Jewish masses, his extensive correspondence and activities show that this break "was far
from complete when it came to feeling a sense of responsibility
for them."[14]

Certainly Friedländer was himself a member of the cultivated
Jewish elite. He attained that status in a situation where, in
Meyer's words, "No one expected that 'old Fritz' [Friedrich the
Great] would adjust the corporate character of the Prussian economic and political system to grant the 'Jewish nation' equality."[15] With the possibility of new beginnings under Friedrich
Wilhelm II, Friedländer became a driving force behind the first
reform efforts of 1787–92. As one of three Jewish deputies
appointed to carry on negotiations with the government, his
writings and collections of documents on behalf of Berlin's Jews
helped do away with the "body tax" and "collective responsibility" but failed in the quest for political liberty and human
rights.[16] Yet this campaign for emancipation came to an end in
1793, a fact that undoubtedly added to the pent-up frustration
behind the appeal to Teller.[17] By the end of the decade
Friedländer was even more outspoken in pursuing these ends. In

13. Lowenstein, *Crisis of Berlin Jewry,* 12.

14. *Ibid.,* 14.

15. Meyer, *Origins,* 65.

16. Lowenstein, *Crisis of Berlin Jewry,* 9; Mordechai Breuer, *German-Jewish History in Modern Times,* vol. 1 of *Tradition and Enlightenment 1600–1870,* ed. Michael
A. Meyer (New York: Columbia University Press, 1996), 344–5.

17. Lowenstein, *Crisis of Berlin Jewry,* 19, writes, "The Enlightenment as a
movement came under attack from many directions. The Prussian government
opposed it as a potentially revolutionary force; the younger generation of poets
and writers like Goethe as well as the Romantic school ridiculed its principles and
its leaders. In the Jewish community the attempt to revive Hebrew as a medium
of Enlightenment petered out as more and more of the Enlightened turned to pure
German. By 1797, the Hebrew-language journal of Enlightened Jewry, *Ha-meassef,*
stopped publication after the number of its subscribers fell to a mere 120."

this context he wrote his *Open Letter* to Teller, not as an official representative of rabbinic authority but as spokesperson for the most influential Jewish families in Berlin.

Friedländer's *Open Letter* is more treatise than epistle. An eighty-six-page treatise in the original German, the appeal provides its readers with a prism of *Haskalah* values within Berlin Jewry. Jews and Christians alike have pilloried his proposal for urging conversion to Protestant Christianity as the vehicle for Jewish emancipation into Prussian civil society. Even with its main qualification (refusing to confess Jesus Christ as Son of God in a Christian sense) few persons then or now can see merit in proposing sham baptism as a means for attaining civil and political rights.

Yet a close reading of Friedländer reveals a remarkable mind in great turmoil. Here was a plea for human understanding and dignity in face of the continued marginalization of German Jewish existence under the growing commercial and political conditions of Berlin. However little merit we may see in linking political rights to church membership, Friedländer's plea deserves our respect. Its dignified tone and rhetoric tell a story that reveals keen intelligence and pride in Jewishness, despite severe quarrels with rabbinic authorities. The document set off a firestorm of some twenty-three pamphlets, plus ten newspaper or journal articles.[18] Despite the work's anonymity, readers quickly associated the plea with Friedländer and his circle,[19] along with the eleven-page essay published anonymously in March 1799, "Political-Theological Task concerning the Treatment of Baptized Jews." Friedrich Schleiermacher, a young hospital chaplain and writer in the Berlin Protestant Church of Teller, was eager to respond to both of these documents.

Historians of religion have long noted how the legacy of Christian anti-Judaism and the rhetoric of religious rivalry play into forces of anti-Semitism. Since antiquity, Christian exclusivism has led to the view that Christian truth has superceded Judaism and rendered it invalid ("supersessionism"). An heir of this tradition,

18. Ellen Littmann, "David Friedländers Sendschreiben an Probst Teller und sein Echo," *Zeitschrift für die Geschichte der Juden in Deutschland* 6 (1935): 92–112.

19. After first denying any involvement, Friedländer acknowledged writing the *Open Letter* in 1819; see Littmann, "David Friedländers Sendschreiben," 93.

Friedrich Schleiermacher (1768–1834) was launching his Berlin career in the late 1790s amid the German Romantics within the transitional era of a post-Mendelssohn generation of Jews. Early on Schleiermacher became a habitué of the Jewish salon of Henriette Herz, which was also frequented by a circle of free-thinking Enlightenment spirits that included educators and high-church officials like Johann Friedrich Zöllner[20] and Teller.[21] Schleiermacher's direct involvement in these issues occurred while finishing *On Religion: Speeches to Its Cultured Despisers*, a classic of modern religious thought that appeared in June 1799.[22] In it, Schleiermacher presents religion as more akin to poetry than to moral code or to formal creed. His insistence that religion first arose from human feeling and intuition of the universe challenged both traditionalists within Protestant Christianity and the widespread proponents of deism, who held that a core of religious truths—belief in God, human virtue, immortality—were self-evident. *On Religion* even questions whether God is a necessary part of religious self-awareness: "Whether we have God as part of our intuition depends upon the direction of our imagination."[23] Inspired by Romanticism, Schleiermacher attacks the Kantian habit of equating morality with religion. He holds that only after religion

20. Like Teller, Johann Friedrich Zöllner (1753–1804), Provost of the Nicolai Church in Berlin after 1788, was also a member of the Upper Consistory Council and of the "Wednesday Society." See Günter Birtsch, "The Berlin Wednesday Society," in *What is Enlightenment? Eighteenth-Century Answers and Twentieth-Century Questions*, ed. James Schmidt (Berkeley: University of California Press, 1996), 238.

21. In a letter to his sister Charlotte (October 26, 1798) Schleiermacher defends his involvement in the Jewish salon against her anxieties and assures her that it will also not impede his external circumstances, since Zöllner and Teller "two of the most prominent clergymen are both often in the Herz' home, indeed not on the intimate and cordial basis as I am. . . ." [*KGA* V.2 *Briefwechsel 1796–1798*, ed. Andreas Arndt and Wolfgang Virmond (Berlin: Walter de Gruyter, 1988), 419]. For the impact of the Jewish salons on Berlin's cultural life, see the recent work by Deborah Hertz, *Jewish High Society in Old Regime Berlin* (New Haven: Yale University Press, 1988); Steven M. Lowenstein, *The Berlin Jewish Community: Enlightenment, Family, and Crisis 1770–1830* (New York: Oxford University Press, 1994) and Peter Siebert, *Der literarische Salon: Literatur und Geselligkeit zwischen Aufklärung und Vormärz* (Stuttgart: Metzler, 1994).

22. Friedrich Schleiermacher, *On Religion: Speeches to Its Cultured Despisers*, ed. and tr. Richard Crouter (Cambridge: Cambridge University Press, 1996).

23. Schleiermacher, *On Religion*, 53.

is experienced within individuals does the force of religion shape institutions and historic communities of faith. Even when muted in *Letters on the Occasion*, Schleiermacher's critical view of Enlightenment religion contrasted with the deism of his more established contemporaries. Yet an underlying Enlightenment sense of liberty (as understood within the French and American revolutions) informed Schleiermacher's overall perspective, which was not unlike the perspective of other participants in the debate.

Schleiermacher's version of supersessionism is reflected in the fifth speech of *On Religion*, where he locates Christianity on a map that contrasts it with Judaic and Hellenic (Greek) religion. There we find the surprisingly illiberal—arguably even blind or bigoted—words: "Judaism is long since a dead religion, and those who at present still bear its colors are actually sitting and mourning beside the undecaying mummy and weeping over its demise and its sad legacy."[24] In a Berlin that had a German-speaking synagogue and communities of practicing Jews, the depiction of Judaism as dead was as prejudicial as it was empirically false. Readers of *On Religion* invariably find the phrase offensive and intellectually baffling. Schleiermacher's correspondence with Henriette Herz, his lifelong soul mate and the leader of a Jewish salon in Berlin, indicates that they conversed long and openly on the status and affairs of Jews in that city.

Of course, intellectual and cultural historians can easily contextualize Schleiermacher's notorious remark about Judaism being dead. To take that approach requires us to become aware of the ambiguous social standing of Berlin's Jews during the same period. The relatively few acculturated Jews, a category that included all of Schleiermacher's Jewish friends, had long endorsed the values of eighteenth-century Enlightenment thought. They tried to follow Mendelssohn's example of thorough acculturation while still (in some fashion) maintaining Jewish practice and observance. A model of character and probity, Mendelssohn is memorialized as the wise Jew in *Nathan the Wise*, written by his Christian friend Gotthold Ephraim Lessing. By and large, Berlin's influential Jewish houses, as centers of culture and of commerce, belonged to the movement of *Haskalah*.

24. *Ibid.*, 113–4.

They wished to shake off the shackles of rigid religious tradition and ensure the possibility of cultural and political life for themselves and their children. However odd it may seem to us today, Schleiermacher's remark about Judaism being dead reflects a belief held by his acculturated Jewish friends—that Halakhic (or observant) Jewish practice and its accompanying ceremonial law were relics of antiquity and impossible to reconcile with modernity.

In the specialist literature on the German Enlightenment, Wilhelm Abraham Teller (1734—1804) is remembered as an eclectic Protestant theologian and an uninspired rationalist. Martin Bollacher has noted that Teller was a minor theologian who would scarcely deserve our attention "if we only judged history by its results and by the power of the written tradition."[25] Yet Teller's contemporaries viewed him as a distinguished churchman, prolific scholar, and one of the most important northern German Protestants to develop an enlightened theology.

Born in Leipzig as the son of a theologian, Teller had all the cultural gifts of language training and historical awareness that typified a German pastor's home. The son's academic and theological career developed early in an exemplary manner. At age twenty-four he was Sunday preacher in Leipzig's Nicolai Church. Three years later, before completing his doctorate, he received a call as general superintendent and professor of theology at the University of Helmstedt. In the terminology of his day, Teller was known as a "neologist," a type of liberal theologian who, like Johann Semler,[26] used the critical tools of ancient languages and history to reconcile Christian dogma with rationality. With the publication of his *Textbook of Christian Faith* (1764) Teller emerged as a controversial figure within orthodox Protestant circles; he was so greatly attacked as a heretic that, in the words of bookseller and poet Friedrich Nicolai's *Memorial Address for Teller* (1807), Teller "feared the worst for his civic honor and for his

---

25. Martin Bollacher, "Wilhelm Abraham Teller: Ein Aufklärer der Theologie," in *Über der Prozeß der Aufklärung in Deutschland im 18. Jahrhundert*, ed. Hans Erich Bödeker and Ulrich Hermannn (Göttingen: Vandenhoeck & Ruprecht, 1987), 40.

26. Johann Salomo Semler (1725–91), a professor of theology in Halle after 1752, is widely recognized as the representative figure within the neologist movement in Protestant theology.

temporal fortunes."[27] His call to Berlin, to the position of Upper
Consistorial Counselor and Provost of the Protestant Church
(1767), rescued Teller from Helmstedt where he had become *persona non grata*. At thirty-four he was by far the youngest member
of the highest religious bureaucracy in the Prussian monarchy, a
post he retained throughout his career.[28] In this capacity Teller
worked toward a reform of the hymnbook, liturgy, and religious
instruction in Berlin. His list of publications kept pace with his
busy life. His *Dictionary of the New Testament for the Explanation of
Christian Doctrine* (1772) went through several editions, and he
produced numerous works in German and Latin on Biblical and
theological issues.

Teller dealt with the notoriously repressive 1788 Wöllner
Edict on religious orthodoxy with moderation, even though he
would come to suffer under the authoritarian regime of
Friedrich Wilhelm II. When Teller voted in favor of a freethinking preacher, an ensuing heresy trial led to his suspension from
his office for several months while his salary went to support the
Berlin insane asylum.[29] As Nicolai noted after Teller's death, the
theologian wrote the "splendid little book," *A Religion of the More
Perfect*, during just this time of troubles, a volume whose scriptural text from 1 Corinthians provided an epigraph for Friedländer's appeal. Religion, as Teller envisaged it, should enable
mankind "to become its own teacher."[30] Martin Bollacher views
Teller's countless sermons, given on numerous occasions, as
examples of a preaching style that bent the German Enlightenment's aristocratic educational tendencies in more egalitarian,
popular directions.[31]

The relevance of Teller's theological liberalism is apparent in
his general championing of religious tolerance, an attitude that
extended to Jews. Only five years younger than Mendelssohn,
Teller enjoyed confidential discussions with the Jewish scholar

27. Bollacher, "Wilhelm Abraham Teller," 42 (citing Friedrich Nicolai,
Gedächtnißschrift auf Dr. Wilhelm Abraham Teller [Berlin/Stettin: n.p., 1807]).

28. Bollacher, "Wilhelm Abraham Teller," 43.

29. *Ibid.*

30. *Ibid.*, citing Teller, *Die Religion der Vollkommnern* (Berlin: Mylius, 1792), 22,
50.

31. *Ibid.*, 47.

and with Johann Joachim Spalding, Nicolai, and other eminent figures in Berlin's exclusive twelve-person Wednesday Society.[32] The group formally debated issues of the day at its regular meetings, and in this setting Mendelssohn issued his *What is Enlightenment?* paper, which provoked Kant's famous response to the same question.[33] Judged alongside his immediate contemporaries, Teller pressed the limits of neology in theology; in his hands the Christian sermon became an occasion not only for addressing social and political issues but also for reflecting on the overall well-being of the family. Unlike his fellow Enlightenment clergyman in Berlin, Johann Joachim Spalding,[34] Teller never overtly took part in efforts to convert Jews to the religion of Jesus Christ. In this respect, and in his theological liberalism, his openness to history and biblical interpretation, his social and ecclesiastical position, and his direct acquaintance with the legacy of Mendelssohn, Teller seemed an appropriate recipient of Friedländer's treatise.

The *Political-Theological Task:* A Satirical Plea for Civil Rights

The first of the translated Judaic essays involves a courageous, anonymously written article called the *Political-Theological Task concerning the Treatment of Baptized Jews.* The essay was published in a scholarly journal, the *Berlin Archive of Time and Taste* (March 1799), which specialized in addressing cultural issues of the day. An outspoken and satirical work, the plea argues for full political rights of all of Prussia's Jews.

Eleven pages in its original format, the work quickly establishes its five central points:

32. Mendelssohn was an honorary member of the society. See Birtsch, "The Berlin Wednesday Society," 241.

33. Moses Mendelssohn, "Über die Frage: was heißt aufklären?" (1784), in Immanuel Kant, *Was ist Aufklärung? Aufsätze zur Geschichte und Philosophie*, 3rd edition, ed. Jürgen Zehbe (Göttingen: Vandenhoeck & Ruprecht, 1985), 129–31.

34. Spalding was obsessed with converting Berlin's philosophical-minded Jews and was the inspiration for Lavater's ill-conceived efforts to convert Mendelssohn. See Alexander Altmann, *Moses Mendelssohn: A Biographical Study* (Tuscaloosa, AL: University of Alabama Press, 1973), 203.

(i) It is a settled and well-understood fact that there is no basic conflict between the Jewish religion and the ability of Jews to engage in full civil rights. (ii) It is absurd to think of the denial of rights to Jews as arising from the charge that they are Christ killers, since it is irrational "to attribute all the vices of posterity to a single evil deed" and also because Christian teaching itself holds that the death of Christ was part of a God-willed plan for salvation. (iii) Hence the denial of such rights must be related to the Jews' allegedly corrupt moral character, and yet, since no impartial observer believes in the latter, this view can only exist as a presumption of the strong, a presumption that arises from a passionately held ill will. (iv) In view of these arguments, why not simply baptize the entire Jewish nation? All one hundred thousand Prussian Jews would thereby be accorded rights and freedoms, and, if the state really views Jews as morally corrupt, that moral corruption would be overcome by "virtue of an incomprehensible supernatural influence." In the tract's words: "Through the mere act of baptism, all these persons would undergo a complete transformation that extends to their innermost being." (34)[35] (v) Although the absurdity of a mass baptism of all Jews may be apparent, it is no more preposterous than what occurs daily where "individual members of this group take the leap into the Christian church." (35) That very act suddenly displaces all limitations that have been put upon them. What seems to work in individual cases, i.e., instant preparation for citizenship that overcomes prior restrictions and moral taint, would have even greater advantages if it were multiplied![36]

The anonymous essay uses clever satire mixed with scorn to highlight the absurdity of anti-Jewish prejudice which is manifest in a host of diverse (and contradictory) arguments and perspectives. Since no one holds that literally all Jews have a bad moral character, this wholesale solution of granting civil rights to the

35. Parenthetical page references in the Introduction refer directly to the texts in this edition.

36. On demographics and the role of social class in conversions, see Breuer, *German-Jewish History,* 250: "Toward the end of the eighteenth century. . .those interested in changing their faith now came increasingly from prosperous and educated circles, especially the families of court Jews."

entire nation at once casts a net that assures the state of at least getting the best and most useful of their numbers. Moreover, by taking this approach one doesn't disturb the Jews' deep internal relations and social bonds that are "the kernel of all virtues, the driving mechanism of all great and good deeds." (35–6) By contrast, if individual conversions continue, "no individual can take this step without tearing a large part of that divine feeling from his heart." (36) There follows a torrent of rhetorical questions that capture the full pathos of a heart-wrenching situation, the social and personal havoc wrought by continued individual conversions. This so compromises one's moral character that the act itself (based on self-will and self-interest) undermines all its apparent advantages. This is the argument, a tour-de-force satire on the plight of Jewish existence.

In its final section, the *Political-Theological Task* details what the state might do to make mass conversion actually work. The biting argument sets forth a series of steps, beginning with the assumption that if all Jews are to enter Christianity simultaneously, they should undergo a period of education (*Bildungszeit*). This will consist of a six-year apprenticeship, during which each convert will learn the sacred truths of Christianity and become Christian, "although his confession of Jesus is earnest in a different way." (38) The state is to withhold the convert's enjoyment of full recognition as a Christian , but the newly admitted, pious, baptized person will have nothing to complain about with regard to the period of waiting. The state will, after the period of waiting, fully accept them; their children will remain Jewish until they come of age but may then qualify for the above plan of education, and a time of deferment will be instituted by the state during which the worrisome features regarding converts who wish to intermarry with Christians will be worked out.

Friedländer's *Open Letter:* A Philosophical Plea for Civil Rights

Friedländer's letter to Teller (variously characterized as desperate, notorious, even infamous) has long been the subject of controversy among interpreters of modern Judaism. In the words of Michael A. Meyer, it has "generally been taken as a renunciation of Judaism; in fact the epistle is largely an apology for it."[37] Much of the document's argument reads like a slightly veiled account of his own experiences,[38] including his long association with Mendelssohn ("this noble man"). A confident, forty-nine-year-old, highly successful silk merchant, Friedländer puts the case for Jewish aspirations in the light of his personal views and deistic philosophy. Liberalism and rationality, which German Jews share with highly educated German Protestants, should become the basis for a new polity. In words that seem almost to echo the American Declaration of Independence, he writes:

> All participants in the sphere of theological sciences of our time, all great teachers who stand at the pinnacle of the Protestant churches don't just admit to themselves but openly and courageously teach that the spirit, the core, the most essential aspect of all religions, can, without exception, only consist of *those truths which lead to the greatest happiness for the whole of mankind* and to the greatest possible education, perfection and development of all their powers. (49, italics added)

Accordingly, revealed religion must be examined, purified, and corrected in light of the principles of natural religion, which Friedländer understands as belief in God, an immaterial human soul, human perfectibility and happiness, immortality, and a sense of responsibility for following God-given moral rules. Emphasizing such common elements while dropping Mendelssohn's insistence on maintaining Jewish ceremonial law (strict Sabbath observance, dietary laws, etc.), would plausibly ensure civil rights, not just for Friedländer but for his children and the other Jewish youth of Berlin. If the biblical Moses were living at this time, Friedlander writes, he too would drop the ceremonial law.

Like the *Theological-Political Task,* Friedländer's sober treatise defends the moral character of Jews against his German audience. Jews may lag behind in intellectual learning, but this is hardly the case on the scale of their moral worth, where they "do

37. Meyer, *Origins,* 70.
38. *Open Letter* (47), "Our innermost conviction tells us. . . . "

not stand one rung lower on the ladder of moral worth than any other learned, refined, and cultivated people." (63) Virtue and vice are "proportionately shared by everyone." (65) Friedländer responds to the age-old European charge that Jews have a dubious moral character with an emotionally charged plea: he has a defender of Judaism, decrying stereotypes of a supposed Jewish criminal mentality and of prejudices related to business, trade, and usury cry out, "Who has given you the right to cast a contemptuous glance at a *bribing Jew,* while closing one's eye to the *bribed judge?*" (66).

But Friedländer's writing becomes more circumspect as he talks about the possibility of Jewish baptism. He first insists on making a distinction between (i) abandoning the religion of his fathers, i.e., the ceremonial laws, and (ii) accepting the Christian religion. To his mind, these actions are *not* linked. To drop the former is not yet to embrace the latter without qualification. Friedländer does not urge that Jews follow a path to full Christian conversion. He reasons, further, that this path is *not* discouraged solely from fear of repercussions within older Jewish ties, i.e., from family or friends, since an enlightened state protects religions "against persecutions based on this change of religion." (69) Rather, Friedlander himself doubts the truth claims of the Christian tradition, and especially its Christ dogma. The same rationalist convictions that prevent him from being a Halakhic Jew also prevent him from being a Christ-centered Christian.

While insisting that he must follow the dictates of reason, Friedländer develops a remarkably cogent account of how a rational approach to the Bible differs from the Bible's Hebraic worldview, which sees God immediately acting in the world. Like his Protestant peers, Friedländer feels it incumbent upon a scholar to relate language study, philosophy, good taste, and human meaning and to use the "advantages of exegesis and hermeneutics" (73) in an effort to penetrate the spirit of the ancient authors. Friedländer weighs the merits of what he calls a "devious path," while expressing some reluctance to mention this topic. (74) He toys with the idea of confessing Jesus as Son of God, while attributing a meaning to the words that differs from Christian usage. But he rejects this path on grounds that, "it would be impure and reprehensible if we used the term *Son of God,* and other similar expressions in a dishonest manner in a wholly different sense than Christians, in order to make them believe that we confessed their dogma." (75) He knows that the inducements to convert are winning the day in his era. "By reciting a few words" a Jew "can secure for himself all the advantages of life, all the civil liberties that the most upright Jew cannot attain through a lifetime of faultless behavior." (76) Yet, for Friedländer, conversions of this type, which are based on rashness and self-interest, cannot serve either the Jews or the state authorities well. In passing the ball to Provost Teller ("Teach us how we can find the way out"[76]) Friedländer seeks endorsement of his own proposal, which would stop short of a convert expressing the words "Son of God," either in a literal or a figurative sense, when undergoing baptism.

Taken as a whole, Friedländer's remarkable letter to Teller is a plea that like-minded Jews might hope to find an institutional base for their beliefs, and thus civil rights for their children, even if they will continue to exist "only as a middle thing between Christians and Jews." (77) The letter ends with a hope "that the true spirit of Protestantism will shelter and protect us and our system within its wider circle." (78)

Schleiermacher's *Letters on the Occasion:* A Theological-Political Intervention

After *On Religion* Schleiermacher next published his little-known, sixty-four-page book with the wordy title, *Letters on the Occasion of the Political-Theological Task and the Open Letter of Jewish Householders*, in July 1799. Kurt Nowak's facsimile edition appeared in East Germany in 1984, shortly before the dismantling of the Berlin wall.[39] Although a near-companion to *On Religion* in its author's early development, the work is little known within English-language scholarship.[40]

39. Kurt Nowak, ed., [Friedrich Schleiermacher], *Briefe bei Gelegenheit der politisch theologischen Aufgabe und des Sendschreibens jüdischer Hausväter* (Berlin: Evangelische Verlagsanstalt, 1984).

40. See Peter Foley, "Der Jude als moralisch zurechnungsfähiger Bürger: Schleiermachers philosophische Erwiderung auf die Frage der Bürgerrechte für Juden," *Theologische Literaturzeitung* 126 (2001) 7/8: 722–34. Schleiermacher's highly rhetorical letters on Judaism are rarely studied as a whole. More often,

Letters on the Occasion is a highly rhetorical piece of writing, worthy of the literary inventions of a Søren Kierkegaard. The anonymous work, in the form of six letters, purports to have been written by "a preacher outside of Berlin" and to have been published by the letters' recipient, a politician involved in making decisions about the Jews. Careful study of the letters conveys the precariousness of Jewish-Christian relations in old Berlin. At the time, Schleiermacher's Jewish acquaintances were deeply alienated from their roots in biblical and Talmudic traditions, and knowledge of Hebrew was diminishing daily. Schleiermacher had promised Henriette Herz that he would write something about Jewish emancipation even as he was working on *On Religion*.[41]

Schleiermacher's March 16, 1799 correspondence shows him discussing the *Political-Theological Task* with Henriette Herz and pledging to respond to it in the Berlin journal where it appeared. In addition, in Schleiermacher's letter to Herz of April 9, 1799, he speaks of receiving and exchanging materials pertaining to Jewish emancipation from Alexander von Dohna.[42] Suddenly, however, a firestorm of debate arose over Friedländer's plea for sham baptism as the entry paper into civil society. In a short time, over

---

interpreters present only selected passages from the letters, and those passages convey a one-sided impression. Dan Cohn-Sherbok (in *The Crucified Jew: Twenty Centuries of Christian Anti-Semitism* [Grand Rapids, MI: William B. Eerdmans, 1992], 138) comments on the Jewish plea to Teller: "Once this Jewish appeal was made public, numerous Christian objections were raised. The theologian Friedrich Schleiermacher, for example, charged the Jewish petitioners with hypocrisy, contending that these individuals were motivated solely by material concerns"; in *German-Jewish History*, 345–6, Mordechai Breuer emphasizes a fundamental contempt of Jews for Christianity that is suggested by a portion of Schleiermacher's letters, as well as the sense that Jews, if converted, would bring the taint of their legalism into the Protestant church, but makes no mention of Schleiermacher's attack upon religious affiliation as a test of citizenship.

41. See Günter Meckenstock, *KGA* I.2, 82–4; Jacob Katz's classic account of Jewish emancipation, *Out of the Ghetto: The Social Background of Jewish Emancipation 1770–1870* (New York: Schocken Books, 1973), 120, reverses the order of publication: "*Speeches on Religion*, published shortly after [Schleiermacher] had taken a stand on the Jewish issue, did a great deal to rescue religion from its subordination to rationalism."

42. *KGA* I.2, 82–3. That Schleiermacher's first fictive letter is dated April 17, two days after he finished writing *On Religion*, further links the two projects. Schleiermacher's longtime friend Alexander von Dohna was a high official in the Prussian government who kept Schleiermacher abreast of political developments.

twenty-three pamphlets and numerous articles in ten different newspapers and magazines appeared in Berlin.[43] Schleiermacher's was but one voice in this maelstrom of opinion. In its day, *Letters on the Occasion* received no more attention than other responses. Schleiermacher had already begun the task of translating Plato's dialogues and so was well aware of the power of both indirect communication and the dialog form as means of discourse on topics that resist simple definition or resolution. Indeed, Schleiermacher's literary skill enabled his fictional persona to raise political questions directly, often in a teasing and playful way, as he addressed the earlier satirical tract and the longer plea of Friedländer. By backdating his six letters from April 17 to July 2, 1799, *Letters on the Occasion* appears to provide a running commentary on the issues relating to Friedländer, Teller, the church, and the Prussian state. It is an open question whether Schleiermacher knew that Friedländer was the author of the *Open Letter*.[44]

43. Ellen Littmann, "David Friedländers Sendschreiben an Probst Teller und sein Echo," *Zeitschriften für die Geschichte der Juden in Deutschland* 6 (1935), 92–112.

44. Most interpreters (e.g., Littmann, Scholtz, and Michael Meyer) think he must have surmised, if not known, that Friedländer was its author. If Schleiermacher did know, his direct contrast of the "splendid Friedländer" (84) against the unknown author of the *Open Letter* is a brilliant and cunning rhetorical subterfuge. Günter Meckenstock, editor of the critical edition of Schleiermacher, urges caution and calls attention to Schleiermacher's two pages of random notes on the emancipation affair in his *Gedanken* ("Youthful Notebooks"). Although the notes name Friedländer, they do so only to contrast the *Sendschreiben* with Friedländer's earlier *Akten-Stücke*. A second entry speculates—one assumes, ironically—that the *Sendschreiben's* author might be a Christian because of its tendency to split hairs in an argument in a crypto-Jesuitical manner. Although Schleiermacher's *Notebooks* comment on the *Political-Theological Task* and Friedländer directly, and show himself acquainted with Friedländer's earlier *Akten-Stücke* on emancipation, Schleiermacher does not directly link Friedländer with the *Open Letter* here, where we might have expected him to do so. Thus data from the *Notebooks* is consistent either with Schleiermacher's knowing or not knowing Friedländer to be author of the *Open Letter*. What is not in doubt, however, is that Schleiermacher does associate Friedländer's prior work with the debate surrounding emancipation; it seems reasonable to conclude that it would have been unlikely if he did not at least surmise that Friedländer also wrote the *Open Letter*. Yet since the Teller letter's dual proposals regarding (i) quasi-conversion and (ii) dropping ceremonial law both went against Friedländer's earlier published views, it would be difficult to connect him directly as author. Besides, the *Open Letter* purports to have had more than a single hand in its making (i.e., it is supposedly from Jewish householders, etc.).

More outspoken on the point than Teller, Schleiermacher sharply opposes the *Open Letter*'s call for entering civil society through Protestant "quasi-conversion." Such a position was anathema to this son of a Jesus-centered Moravian piety. Schleiermacher's letters criticize this aspect of the proposal as unneeded and demeaning. But his position attacking a religious test for citizenship is clearly set forth in the "First Letter":

> Reason demands that all should be citizens, but it does not require that all must be Christians, and thus it must be possible in many ways to be a citizen and a non-Christian—which surely any number already have become—and to discover among them that way that is suited to our situation and the case at hand; that is the task that no one can escape who wishes to speak openly about this matter and that thus far has not been treated such that one might let it rest as settled. (85)[45]

Being Christian, or indeed following any other religion, is by no means a necessary condition for full and effective citizenship. Here Schleiermacher speaks directly to the underlying issue behind the polemical satire of the *Political-Theological Task*. Agreeing with that document, he playfully assaults the "lazy reason" of statecraft, which avoids thinking of new solutions and falls back on old, settled understandings as a (false) means of solving problems: "How should it not be a case of irresponsible cowardice to give up on that very thing that is known to be not only desirable but necessary?" (85) *Letters on the Occasion* seeks to tease state policy-makers out of their laziness by presenting some useful new ideas. He attempts, first, to meet the standard political and economic objections to emancipation. The state cannot withhold civil rights solely on the economic grounds that, in its present arrangement, it receives "protection money" (*Schutzgeld*) from Jews, a view of an unenlightened government that Schleiermacher rejects. But, second, he also hastens to critique the age-old Christian European dogma that "the inner corruption of the Jews" makes it "dangerous to accept them into civil society," (87) a dogma that he finds widespread among German political elites.

---

45. This position is consistent with arguments about the separation of church and state in *On Religion*.

Schleiermacher's Second Letter notes the tension between Friedländer's apparent aversion to Christianity and his desire to embrace the larger tradition.[46] The *Open Letter* takes the contradictory stand of seeking to undercut Christian truth while simultaneously desiring to join the Protestant church. While Friedländer insists on the incompatibility of modern reason with the Christological dogma, Schleiermacher is concerned to defend a rational Christ-centered interpretation of his religion.[47] Although Schleiermacher does not comment directly upon the *Open Letter*'s desire to avoid the phrase "Son of God" in making a Christian confession, one can assume that he believed the strategy was duplicitous.

In Schleiermacher's *Third Letter*, which he dates as May 2, his voice takes on a decidedly harsh tone. The ruse of backdating, which conceals the fact that he had already read Teller's response, enables him to offer criticism without crossing paths with Teller directly. As a convinced Christian, Schleiermacher takes conversion of Jews "to be the worst thing that can happen." (95) He contends that the conversion of Jews—even if not harmful to the state—will surely do harm to the Christian church. "By far most of those whom we can expect among us will be the sort of persons who are wholly indifferent towards anything having to do with religion." (96) They are against its moral customs, ruled by worldly sentiments, or else are convinced Kantians who equate their own morality with religion. Schleiermacher's roots in Moravian pietism and in an experiential faith shine forth clearly. The tendency toward external adherence to religion was only aided and abetted by political agreements like the Peace of Westphalia (1648), which re-enforced the territorial religious settlement of the Peace of Augsburg (1555). Here Schleiermacher argues against

46. "All of this taken together brings me to the thought that the author cannot be serious even by half in the way he proposes conversion to Christianity; rather that his intention is only to proceed in such a way as to make it obvious that such a half-way transition is the most that could be undertaken by a reasonable and educated man, quite apart from the fact that one does not wish to require anything of the kind. This secret meaning will satisfy the Jewish nation, which is so clever in matters of interpretation, whereas the letter and the appearance of peace and dignity is for the Christians; the former to embarrass them, the latter to keep them in a good mood." (92–3)

47. Schleiermacher, *On Religion*, Speech 5, 115–8.

Friedländer's popular Kantianism, in which natural religion and truths of reason equate morality with religion. He chides the *Political-Theological Task's* call for a time of education (*Bildungszeit*). Even if the latter extended twenty years, it would remain inadequate. Schleiermacher's reasoning on this point is curious. He makes it sound as if religious choice is determined organically by the accidents of birth, never to be altered or changed.

> It is impossible for anyone who really has a religion to accept another one; and if all Jews were most excellent citizens, not a single one of them would be a good Christian; but they would bring along a great many peculiarly Jewish elements in their religious principles and convictions that, just for this reason, are anti-Christian. (98)

Schleiermacher's romantic organicism reflects the tension in his thought between this essentialist dimension of religious adherence and the truly Enlightenment endorsement of human rights for Jews. On the one hand, he removes any religious test for full legal rights and citizenship. On the other hand, he finds it abhorrent that one might casually swap religions as if trading on the commodities market. Schleiermacher takes the core theological values of Christianity and Judaism to be incompatible. Hence he remarks with sarcasm that a "judaizing Christianity is the true disease with which we should infect ourselves!" (98) This incompatibility of Torah-based religion with its daughter faith was resolved in the New Testament letters of Paul, which defend the freedom of the Christian life against undue emphasis on law. Far from welcoming Jews into its midst, the Church should resist this process, for if "it endures this all-the-more decadent governmental courtesy even longer, it will pay, much too dearly indeed, for this politeness with its complete ruin." (99) For Schleiermacher, Jews are not morally tainted so much as they are legalistically burdened by an outmoded religious practice. Of course, Teller has also jettisoned the Halachic traditions of Judaism. But Schleiermacher worries that law is a definitive feature that will continue to shape the tradition.

Yet arguments against Jews as Jews are rejected in the theologian's fourth letter. He responds to the age-old charge of Jewish moral taint and corruption among Jews by acknowledging that moral corruption also occurs among his own people. "Who would wish to deny that our own common people are well-inclined to deceive foreigners?" (104) He also defends the social cohesion that German society recognized and feared in the Jewish community.[48] In addition to giving up ceremonial law and the hope for a messiah (both elements that Friedländer was willing to cast away) Schleiermacher's view requires that Jews "constitute a special ecclesiastical society." (105) In effect, he goes beyond Teller's desire for a more uniform religious body to argue for a proto-reform movement among German Jews. This "altered Judaism" would be capable of coexisting with the church as a state-recognized Judaism that embodies the two prior conditions of (i) subordinating ceremonial law to German civil law and (ii) giving up the hope in a messiah. Full citizenship of Jews in Schleiermacher's Prussia thus requires a degree of subordination to state sovereignty, which in turn cares for the well-being of recognized religious societies. By avoiding the need to unite with the church to ensure Jewish civil liberties, Schleiermacher believes he has improved upon Friedländer's proposal. He writes as if an "evil demon" had driven a desperate Friedländer to turn to a bond with the church to obtain a secure place in society. But if rights could be assured short of converting to Christianity, that would be a gain for both Jew and Christian. Putting baptism aside, the "Fourth Letter" unambiguously endorses both of the Judaic documents.[49] Thus Schleiermacher, as Christian theologian who takes a strongly anti-Judaic line on religious grounds and whose *On Religion* had maintains that "Judaism is dead,"

---

48. "Only for this reason do the Jews separate themselves from other fellow citizens, so that when the time of departure comes, they may be as little entangled as possible, while being bound together as much as possible." (104) The passage seems to anticipate that Jews may eventually be forced to emigrate from their home locations within the German provinces.

49. "Thus once one has wholly excluded its false elements, the *Open Letter* contains everything that the state can demand from the Jews and is the true codex of a new Judaism, capable and worthy in every way of political existence." (106)

"You see how little I am against the *Open Letter* when I allot it this place! I see the *Task* and the *Open Letter* as necessary and complementary pieces and believe that, taken together, both contain everything that the Jews have to do for their benefit: the former indirectly by provoking the state to depart from its accustomed way; the latter directly by opening a new way to it." (106)

turns in the *Letters on the Occasion* to give full support to Friedländer's central demand for civil and political rights.

In his sixth and last letter, dated May 30, Schleiermacher's fictionalized clergyman acknowledges Teller's response to Friedländer, which had appeared in the meantime. He views the elderly church statesman's work with respect, as providing "several significant suggestions."[50] Read somewhat between the lines, the Schleiermacher letter signals its readers that its author is more respectful of Jewish aspirations than were the majority of voices among Berlin clergy. Overall, the *Letters on the Occasion* challenges Teller's acquiescence with regard to Jews converting to the church and directly calls for the state to drop the test of religious confessions as a requirement for political freedom. In his recent article on this debate and its participants, "Are Christians the Only Good Citizens?" Bernd Oberdorfer wonders whether the entire episode is a promising moment in the development of peaceful coexistence between Jew and Christian or whether it is the first step toward the Nuremberg laws.[51] At least Schleiermacher, as an unencumbered young theologian whose reputation was yet to unfold, answered Oberdorfer's title question resoundingly in the negative.[52]

Teller's *Response to the Open Letter:* A Friendly Yet Cautious Rejoinder

In their endorsements of the Enlightenment, and in social standing, Friedländer as a Jew and Teller as a Christian have much in common. Friedländer did Teller the honor of quoting from Paul's

50. "Without hesitation he presents his private opinion to an audience with which he has such diverse relationships, and with rare resignation he casts aside all worldly considerations in order to clarify, according to his insight, only that about which he's been asked." (112)

51. Bernd Oberdorfer, "Sind nur Christen gute Bürger? Ein Streit um die Einbürgerung der Juden am Ende des 18. Jahrhunderts: Verheißingsvoller Ansatz für ein friedliches Zusammenleben oder erster Schritt zu den Nürnberger Gesetzen?" *Kerygma und Dogma* 44 (October–December 1998): 290–310.

52. Schleiermacher's subsequent political realism and progressive temperament was profoundly shaped by Prussia's experience with the aftermath of the French Revolution. See Richard Crouter, "Schleiermacher and the Theology of Bourgeois Society: A Critique of the Critics," *Journal of Religion* 66, no. 3 (July 1986): 302–23.

letter to the Corinthians as epigraph, thus alluding to Teller's book about the religion of the "more perfect," i.e., Enlightened Christians. Whether Teller knew that Friedländer was the author of the *Open Letter* cannot be determined with certainty. Throughout his response, Teller writes with respect and courtesy and seeks to establish rapport with his Jewish petitioners while not glossing over differences.

Teller begins his response to the author of the *Open Letter* by pointing to their many areas of agreement. He is sympathetic with the *Open Letter*'s points about the inadequacy of Hebrew for expressing abstract thought, and about the difficult historical oppression of the Jewish people. On the issue of alleged moral taint, Teller responds by citing Paul's teaching that "all are sinners." He also agrees with Friedländer's account of Moses' having given the ceremonial laws, though not as being essential for all times. Even the Ten Commandments, Teller says, were more a matter of governing civil society under God as direct ruler than prescriptions for morality. This situation appears to be acceptable to Teller, since he agrees with Friedländer that the "permanently valid" commandments "are self-evident when the human being has already been trained for higher morality." (118) In keeping with the neologism of his day, Teller supports the view that the higher moral truths of the Bible can be inferred by natural reason. By contrast, a case like Sabbath observance—which has direct consequences for organizing political and social existence—"is in no way an essential requirement of the religion." (119)

In beginning his argument, Teller takes delight in noting Friedländer's Jewish self-criticism and apparent revisionism, and his position that the elements of nonmoral and ritual Jewish practice ("ceremonial laws") have become superfluous as a result of the Jewish nation's greater development and embracing of reason.[53] Well-trained in Protestant exegesis of the Old Testament, Teller cites those biblical texts that represent the strata of anti-temple, anti-ritual, and anti-sacrificial in the prophetic traditions, including the Wisdom of Solomon, Ecclesiastes, Isaiah, and Ezekiel, which he freely quotes and paraphrases.

---

53. "You are not further obliged to those laws, yet are indeed obliged to acknowledge the eternal truths of reason that underlie the true dignity of humanity." (119)

But Teller acknowledges that the historical and rational character of biblical revelation has come of age through the legacy of Mendelssohn, who is cited directly along with notables within the Jewish community, including Bloch, Herz, Davidson, Euchel and Bendavid, in addition to Friedländer. Teller locates the current moment in history, in which he takes "heartfelt delight," in an even longer stream of tradition, which he dates from the purer representations of Judaism in antiquity—the Essenes or the highly hellenized appropriations of the tradition by Josephus and Philo.

Only when Teller is one-third into his response does he begin to criticize conversion to Christianity as the means for achieving the notable political ends of an acculturated and rational form of Jewish existence. Here Teller tells his interlocutors that he sided against Lavater's efforts to convert Moses Mendelssohn and suggests that the memory and historical work of Mendelssohn "will immediately lose all influence among his fellow believers" if conversions should follow. Instead, Teller appears to argue for a delay of such conversions "for the longest time possible" until in God's good time "all Israel shall be saved" by joining in the fold.[54] Even more personally Teller asks:

> Will you not thereby lose all effective power over the mass of your local and foreign fellow brethren to the same convictions of a more genuine and more reasonable religiosity? Who is able to decide whether it is not the plan of the Eternal One to use you to that end? (124)

Citing the *Open Letter* directly on the point of requiring civil rights immediately upon conversion, Teller declines to speak for the state about what, in addition to giving up the ceremonial law, it might require for citizenship,. He cites a case in England where an anonymous document called *Policy of the Metropolis* argues that the special laws of Judaism are a hindrance to full civic life and arouse the suspicions of the state.

For reasons of Jewish self-preservation, Teller thus argues against conversion of the Jews ("I am just not a maker of proselytes"). At the same time, he is quick to state that, "Nonetheless, I give you my hand and my voice most willingly as a member and

54. Citing Paul's Letter to the Romans 11:26.

even as a teacher of the Protestant church . . . if you join the same church and wish to confess to the Christianity purified from the time of the Reformation onward." (126) Teller does not accept the *Open Letter's* position that giving up ceremonial laws and accepting the Christian religion are "two entirely different matters." For him, the rationale for ceasing to practice the binding regulation of Torah flows directly into the new life rendered possible by Jesus Christ. For Teller, like Schleiermacher, this is the central teaching of Paul and the New Testament.

The Berlin Provost appears to grasp correctly that the proposal before him does not seek to establish yet another (Enlightenment) sect within Judaism but rather to bring Jews into the Protestant Church as a form of religion that is taken to be purer and more tolerant than other parties within Christianity. Teller thus acknowledges the specific point that Friedländer has asked him to clarify: What would be the appropriate meaning of the term "Son of God" in such a confession of faith for enlightened Jews joining Protestantism? In effect, the *Open Letter* is asking for the definition of a minimalist or unitarian view of Christ.

Teller begins with what first appears to be veiled language. He does, however, state the view that as much as he also endorses a pure undisguised religion (one that is rational and based on enlightened morality), religion that is wholly removed from the senses cannot be sustained among humans in the long run. In effect, Teller warns his Jewish interlocutors about the perils of having a philosopher's religion. He gives a culinary analogy— the need to be careful about the ingredients added to this dish (pure moral religion) so as not to ruin its enjoyment. Such observations prepare Teller to argue on behalf of the importance of the physical acts of Christian rituals, especially that of baptism (which the *Open Letter*, in some fashion, also envisages) and of the sacrament of communion, in which the benefits of Christ are transmitted to a believer. Because of his firm belief in the efficacy of Christian ritual, Teller cannot release his interlocutors "from believing," i.e., from making some commitment to the underlying truth and experience of Christianity. In making this argument, Teller observes that even Friedländer has acknowledged that truths of reason can be strengthened by historical truths and that a distinction between rational and historical truth should not be viewed as absolute.

All of the preceding arguments bring Teller to the direct asser-
tion that, as a minimum, to become a Christian is to "accept
Christ as the *founder of the better moral religion.*" (131) Something
like that formulation would be considered a fundamental teaching, and can be distinguished from the sorts of dogmas that from
time to time take on hardened or corrupted and distorted mean-
ings. Although expressed in hardened form, such dogmas may
"be for each person what they can be, as long as one does not
impose them in a domineering way on others." (132) To para-
phrase Teller by using his own New Testament formulations:
There is some yoke involved, some standard of belief that is
required within Protestantism, though rightly understood along
with Jesus' words in Matthew 11:29–30: "My yoke is easy and my
burden is light." If a further kind of confession of Christian belief
is needed, Teller does not recommend the Apostles' Creed but
rather cites passages from Ephesians, Chapter 4, on the unity of
body, spirit, Lord, and Christ, and continues by suggesting that
the formulae for Jewish baptism should be the same as those
used by Peter and Paul in the book of Acts. Thus a reluctant
churchman who speaks against conversion provides a direct
answer to Friedländer's query. Teller refuses to entertain or
accept a version of Christian faith that would differ from that
which he himself espouses within his own community.

Having dealt with the substance of the *Open Letter,* the final
third of Teller's response speaks to the likelihood and possible
consequences of the state's acting on Friedländer's proposal.
Although Teller's remarks are merely a private judgment, he
offers the opinion that fellow clergy would set a good example by
acting with toleration toward these new converts, much as they
have done in relations with the Moravian Brethren. Of course,
just which and how many civil rights the state might be apt to
grant based upon such a Christian confession "belongs in a completely different forum." (137) Hence Teller's argument ends with
deferential reflection on the ongoing relationship between church
and state. He recognizes that state interest and state welfare can
and do often intervene in religious affairs and communities. In
light of then recent church-state and inter-church relations,
including those between the Lutheran and Reformed branches of
Protestantism in Germany, Teller acknowledges the state's final
authority in such questions. Early on in his response Teller had

decried the radical deism of Thomas Paine and this position's influence within the French Revolution. In the polity of Prussia Teller's deism, far from providing a revolutionary platform for liberty, fraternity, and equality of all peoples, acknowledges the preeminence of the state that he serves in his official capacity as churchman.

Richard Crouter

TWO JUDAIC VOICES
(MARCH AND APRIL, 1799)

Anonymous:
Political-Theological Task concerning the Treatment of Baptized Jews[1]

A society of friends, invigorated by patriotism and an interest in eternal truths, wishes a serious response to the following question and would consider itself fortunate if it succeeded in drawing the attention of some good minds to a subject that seems to be of not inconsiderable political as well as a theological interest.

One can take it as a given: In our times of general enlightenment the limitation in regard to civil freedoms and rights under which the Jewish nation still lives in a great part of Germany has nothing to do with the essential characteristics of its religion. It has been agreed, said hundreds of times, and demonstrated with unimpeachable proof that neither in that ancient faith nor in the ceremonies that it prescribes nor in the doctrines that it advances is the least thing contained that imparts to its adherents an incapacity for applying their physical as well as spiritual powers in the best interests of the state and, as a result of this, for sharing equally with their uncircumcised brothers in the general well-being of society.

In addition, it would be nonsensical to believe that the nations, in putting that poor nation under this mortifying pressure, merely bring into play the feeling of retaliation on account of their forefathers' mistreatment of the founder of the great religious society. Given the level of culture of which the end of the 18th century partakes, one does not venture to entertain such a horrid and ridiculous thought. When Moses portrays with fervor an enraged God, the height of premonition he allows himself is that the sins of the parents extend to the third and fourth generations. It is also probably not unusual for the life of a sinner to extend over three or four generations, and the sight of his descendants' suffering adds greatly to a sense of being punished justly

1. "Politisch-theologische Aufgabe über die Behandlung der jüdischen Täuf-linge," *Berlinisches Archiv der Zeit und ihres Geschmacks* 5, Teilband 1 (Berlin, 1799): 228–89, reprinted in Schleiermacher, *KGA* I.2: 373–80.

for sins one committed. But to bear a grudge endlessly against all descendants of the wicked ones, to let the most distant and least guilty descendants do penance for a crime committed by their forebears, is as inhumane as it is senseless; it is scarcely to be presumed of any rational creature gifted with human feeling, unless one takes actual delight in the torment of others and welcomes every sort of reason that is pulled out of thin air to be unashamedly happy about this evil enjoyment. As already mentioned, such a thing is least to be expected at the end of the 18th century.

This is not even to mention that the momentous deed in Jerusalem can appear neither as sin nor as a crime even to the adherents of the great religion, since, according to their own doctrine, this deed, destined from time immemorial for the salvation of the world, necessarily had to happen. And even if the means of which the creator availed himself in carrying this out were undertaken from impure zeal and not for the sake of its final purpose, they would then at most deserve sympathy, scarcely hatred and persecution; but their descendants surely ought to be able to make the most well-founded claim to recognition by the whole world, whose well-being is the work of their fathers, even if it happened inadvertently. The children of a physician who allowed a rich man to die prematurely have probably never had to suffer persecution from such a man's formerly indigent heirs.

When, apart from this, the most enlightened and best educated states nevertheless continue to hold their unbaptized members in oppression and exclude them from so many of the rights and freedoms given to the worst of their subjects, the cause must not be in the nature of their distinctive religion. It lies neither in their not confessing Jesus nor in the expectation of a messiah whom few truly still await. Rather it must be sought more deeply in their character, their convictions, their education; in a certain ill humor, perversion, uselessness of their physical and mental capabilities, on account of which they are totally unreceptive to the enjoyment of those civil blessings. One must assume that through an inherited mixture of bodily fluids their physical powers have been weakened or numbed; that through a manner of instruction and education transmitted by their forebears their higher spiritual capacities have been mutilated and have taken a contrary direction; and that through inherited convictions, maxims taken in with their mothers' milk, and social intercourse, their inclinations and feelings, especially in matters social, have become perverse, corrupt, and highly damaging. Thus with all this taken together they are thoroughly incapable of fulfilling the duties demanded by the state and consequently also incapable of the correlative enjoyment of the rights vouchsafed by the state for this fulfillment.

The society of friends is far removed from viewing this hypothetically assumed opinion about the Jewish nation as assuredly true. But it still remains the only reason on the basis of which something reasonable, lawful, and fair can be grasped in the oppressive and derogatory conduct of the majority of humans towards their fellow brothers. Without this opinion this conduct can only be considered by an impartial observer as a presumption of the stronger party or as a consequence of an ignorant ill will that is just as passionate as it is contrary to any sound rules of governing. Just how little either view can be attributed to the wise rulers and peoples of Europe needs no extensive commentary.

This being assumed, the question thus arises: How would it be if the entire Jewish nation all at once made the decision to be baptized? Would the state possibly act wisely if it incorporated those hundred thousands, who according to the previous assumption would be useless and probably even harmful, immediately after they completed the ceremony? Would it act wisely if, ignoring all of their previous incapacities, it bestowed on them all rights and freedoms? Are these only proper as a necessary recompense to its naturally Christian members for their services rendered to society and which are likewise impossible for those artificial Christians to achieve? Would the state conduct itself equitably if it were thus to withhold the many types of civil enjoyment from worthy subjects capable of civil pursuits and burdens, while bestowing them on a crowd of the useless and unworthy? Or might it be more likely for the state to believe it could gloss over this purposeless squandering by thinking that by virtue of an incomprehensible supernatural influence, through the mere act of baptism, all these persons would undergo a complete transformation that extends to their innermost being? That all at once their muscles would receive more strength, their fluids a better mixture, their head and their heart, their modesty and morality, their convictions and inclinations a more favorable turn toward the fulfillment of civil duties?

From this question springs forth another, whose answer has even more difficulty: If, as will probably never happen, the entire Jewish nation does not renounce its faith publicly but if, as occurs daily, only individual members of this group take the leap into the Christian church, how is it wise and fair and advantageous to release them one minute after their baptism from all the limitations that up to then were based on reason, humanity, and the needs of the state and to grant them all the rights and enjoyments of those who were born as Christian subjects?

The task of answering this question is even more difficult, since, on the one hand, the disadvantage to the state in granting wasteful favors to individuals seems less great, but, on the other hand, wisdom, prudence, and advantage to the state resist such individual favors more resolutely than universal ones that might be accorded an entire people.

For, first of all, one cannot at all assume that the universality of that misanthropic claim about the unsuitability of the whole nation tolerates no exceptions and that, with all prejudice set aside, no single worthy and educated members might be found among this people who are wholly capable of fulfilling all civil duties. The Christian state manifestly acquires these persons when it takes the whole people at once into its bosom; the number of these individual exceptions is perhaps larger than the opposing prejudice imagines, and they are also perhaps so important in inherent value that they offset the disadvantage of their brothers' uselessness. But in regard to individual renegades, what compensates the active citizens for the harm of withdrawing the [exclusive] enjoyment [of civil rights] from them and squandering that enjoyment undeservedly on those others? Unless those very individuals would be among those exceptions and would be precisely the most active, capable, best-educated, wisest, and most virtuous of their people! Whether, indeed, this is the case, experience must determine!

Second, if the entire people throws itself into the arms of its Christian brothers, the moral relationship in which its members stand in relation to one another remains undisturbed. The devotion of parents to their children, and children to their parents; the feelings of marital love and of friendship; the trust among relatives, teachers, benefactors—these tender feelings, the nobility of humanity, the social bonds, the kernel of all virtues, the driving mechanism of all great and good deeds remain undisrupted. Based on better or more clever insight, the families have altered their opinion about certain doctrines related to deity and have expressed this change publicly, but they continue just as before to practice those noble feelings of humanity that stand in such a precise relationship to honest convictions. The inner person remains unharmed, and so long as this is the case, all external and so easily alterable circumstances are of little significance. These are transformed, and everything good and excellent is to be expected from an incorruptible man who expresses himself in deeds. Thus the state can perhaps, indeed probably will one day—even if it takes generations—see a fruitful increase of capable and useful citizens among the newly acquired, morally unweakened people by extending the limits of its activity, by giving its powers more latitude and giving its state of affairs a different direction, and by seeking, through social intercourse and association, to make them resemble its Christian members. Such an increase has to be no inconsiderable gain for the state.

But for the individual converts? No individual can take this step without tearing a large part of that divine feeling from his heart. Before long he robs his parents of their joy and support, robs his children of their educator, robs his marriage partner of his heart, and almost always robs his friends of their love and his benefactors of their thanks. He knows that now the bond between him and these people is dissolved, knows that they loathe him, that he often makes them unhappy, that not seldom he intends to make them unhappy. Thus stripped of ethical feeling—even more than stripped, equipped with the opposite feelings—he steps before the altar and embraces the Savior. What does the state have to expect from such a degenerate? A good father in that person who, for the sake of a couple of lustful nights, delivered his family members into disconsolateness? A good mother in that person who, perhaps in order to be able to set a better table or nurture her vanity more lavishly, scorns and teases her own people, and even insults and curses them on account of their genuine piety? Will the fulfillment of duties towards the abstract object called the state lie burning in that person's heart who recklessly tramples on the most natural inclinations innate in every human, in almost every animal? Will a sense of empathy with unfortunate neighbors glow in the breast of one who scornfully laughs at the wailing of his own flesh and blood? Will laws and a sense of justice be revered in the bosom of one who, for the sake of pursuing dishonesty and profit in places where he was formerly not allowed to stay, makes light of what would be right for his family members?

Of course, truth is a free realm that must stand open to everyone, whose entrance cannot be justly blocked by any state. To be sure, truth is the most important treasure of a human being; all objects of desire must yield to its charm. To profess truth and to do so loudly is the primary duty for which no sacrifice, even life itself, is too great; and the one who, out of respect for truth, voluntarily partakes of the blissful enjoyment of such fine sensitivity, the one who, filled with its divinity, renounces the sense of delight in parents, relatives, friends, and benefactors in order to pay homage publicly only to it, is a worthy martyr of reason. Admiration of such a person's strength of mind as well as the love and esteem of all his impartial communal brothers because of his righteous and virtuous convictions—the immediate and necessary accompaniments of the devotion to truth—won't escape his notice. Nor will it escape the notice of all his religious brethren, even if they have the conversion of just a single such virtuous figure to point to during an entire century.

However, such admiration and love is really the only thing with which someone who confesses truth must content himself. As soon as he makes a claim to monetary reward, to liberation from accustomed limitations, to acquisition of new rights, the purity, together with the greatness of his action, is cast aside. He sinks down to the depraved class of people who sacrifice themselves and their worth for small restitution and barter away the feeling for eternal truths for lower sensual enjoyment. No one guarantees that under changed situations and circumstances, if he does not find the rate of exchange of the religious belief he just left more advantageous, he would not once again exchange this religious belief without any scruples, under many sorts of pretexts.

And even if this misgiving does not affect a single authentic convert, he still can hardly escape the ill repute of the world, as if he were, in the customary manner, just making profit from the truth. It is not only incumbent on him, as for every person of virtue, to avoid this appearance, but also the duty of the state to rescue him from it. Indeed, such an action is for the state's own sake, so that it might not appear, first, to crave proselytes and, second, to draw to itself through the magnitude of its reward a mob of useless hypocrites who, in the enjoyment of civil privileges based on civil attributes, do such injury to the truly deserving members.

Assuming the argument as established to this point, the correctness or falsity of which is now presented for judgment, the society of friends desires the determination of the following question: Would every Christian state not act more advantageously, wisely, and judiciously if it were to proceed more effectively in dispensing civil well-being to baptized persons? And, indeed, in the following ways:

1. Assure a freely accepted Christian religion to every member of the Jewish nation without any difficulties; but

2. for a period of time consider him as dependent, as a pupil still in the years of formal education.[2] This would be not exactly an education in the propositions and doctrines of Christianity, which with average mental ability one can learn to recite in a certain number of days, but an education of the soul, of convictions, of a way of thinking with all the qualities that make one worthy of participating in civic rights and freedoms, from which, because he lacked the former qualities, the newcomer had hitherto been excluded. Such education, which consists of a complete reorientation of the inner person, is a matter by no means easy to learn: It will only be gradually acquired through long and sustained practice. Then it would have to follow that

3. this period of education[3] has to be prescribed for at least six years, during which time the sacred elements of Christianity are accessible to him and he is obliged to occupy himself with them but is prevented from entering into the characteristic rights and freedoms already enjoyed by educated Christians. Although his confession of Jesus is earnest in a different way for him, he is fully a Christian before God and his conscience but, in view of his external circumstances, not yet before the state. For the state, he is a person who, situated in Christianity, seeks to make himself worthy of the state; an apprentice, who strives to accommodate himself to the master's prerogatives; he is not a convalescent but

2. [Eds.] *Bildung.*
3. [Eds.] *Bildungszeit.*

ANONYMOUS: *POLITICAL-THEOLOGICAL TASK*   39

one who is recovering, from whom the careful physician wisely withholds the free enjoyments of a healthy person out of worry over a setback. The pious baptized person has nothing to complain about with respect to this withholding—for whom it is and must only be a matter of truth and of union with Jesus.

4. Following these extended years of apprenticeship he would have to be viewed as a politically complete Christian and as a full participant in the enjoyments and rights of citizenship. It would be unjust to dispute his right to them, since with the greatest probability one can assume that he has acquired the capacity for this new status.

5. That which holds good for baptized individuals would also apply to their children. Those not yet of age in civil society must by no means be taken up into the bosom of the Christian church; further, the parents have neither the right nor the authority to tear them away from the religion of their birth and at will to force another one upon them. By contrast, children already of age would in a natural way, as persons in their own right, have to undergo the predetermined time of education if they wished to follow the example of their parents.

6. Finally, a time of deferment would have to be instituted, only after which marriage of both men and women is permitted, for allowing it immediately following baptism carries with it two concerns: First, the naturally Christian half of the marriage might be corrupted by the newly acquired half; and, second, not only would children born during the time of education bring a Jewish kind of physical and mental idiosyncrasy into the world, but also the instruction they receive from the baptized mother or father would not be adequate for pure Christian instruction, i.e., not adequate for future citizenship.

By treating baptized persons according to this standard, the society of friends believes that the state has two advantages. First, those who submit to the norm and, despite these limitations, enter into the bosom of the Christian church are certainly persons of truth who do not pursue momentary enjoyments to satisfy vain desires or a base instinct. Instead, they do so that they may follow their better insight and satisfy the voice of conscience, burst the powerful bonds with which nature has shackled them to so many things. Second, the state will thereby be universally rescued from the great reproach of inconsistency in view of its conduct toward the Jewish nation; for it does in fact truly remain inconsistent to withhold from hundreds of thousands the duties and rights of citizens (unless for the reason that their entire inner nature makes them wholly incapable of these rights) while it in turn immediately bestows on them those benefits in their entirety as soon as they have undergone a ceremony lasting a few minutes, which can have no influence on their inner transformation!

David Friedländer:
Open Letter to His Most Worthy, Supreme Consistorial Counselor and Provost Teller at Berlin, from some Householders of the Jewish Religion[1]

> *But when the more perfect comes, the imperfect will pass away. When I was a child, I spoke like a child, I thought like a child, I reasoned like a child; when I became a man, I gave up childish ways.*[2]
> *1 Corinthians 13:10–1*

Printed with approval of the censor after a question was addressed to me, and thus also with my permission. My response will similarly appear in print as soon as I have been able to think through and consider the matter in light of its importance amid many sorts of business and interruptions.   Teller

Most Worthy Sir,
Venerable Friend of Mankind

Permit us, most worthy Sir, who are not members of your church but are no less trusting than your most grateful pupils, to request from you instruction, counsel, and support in the greatest and most holy affair of man, which is religion.

Not vanity, which wants to create a stir; not a doubting heart, which wants to be free from the embarrassing condition of inde-

---

1. *Sendschreiben an Seine Hochwürden, Herrn Oberconsistorialrath und Probst Teller zu Berlin, von einigen Hausvätern jüdischer Religion* (Berlin: August Mylius, 1799), reprinted in Schleiermacher, *KGA* I.2: 381–413.

2. [Eds.] The motto of the *Open Letter*, 1 Corinthians 13:10–1, is taken directly from the book by Abraham Teller, *Die Religion der Vollkommnern* (Berlin, 1792); the New Testament citation of the *Open Letter* retains Teller's emendation of the Pauline passage by using the comparative ("more perfect"), an idea that reflects the Enlightenment theologian's liberal philosophy of human perfectibility.

cision; not aversion to effort and self-examination, which so happily seeks refuge in authority; much less any other ignoble intent leads us to your seat of learning. Bestow on us, noble Sir, a favorable hearing. Just as we might rightly expect in this affair a thorough and comforting judgment from your mind, so in composure and trust we await from your heart the announcement of the step that should be taken with bold thoughtfulness.

We were born of Jewish parents and reared in the Jewish religion. Our education had nothing distinguishing it from that of our comrades. Already in childhood the Talmud was put in our hands as a textbook, perhaps even earlier than sacred scripture. The religion that was taught to us, then, was full of mystical principles. The story of the primeval world was full of secrets, dark, incoherent; the events were foreign and, down to the last shades of meaning, so dissimilar to the occurrences of the world in which we lived that they seemed almost unbelievable. Characters, states of mind, and feelings of people who emerge in sacred scripture not only were puzzling for us in matters of expression but also, for the most part, stood in contrast to our feelings, expressions, and ways of acting. The ceremonial laws were observed with worrisome precision in the paternal household. These alienated us in the circle of everyday life; as empty customs without any further influence on our other preoccupations, they had no other effect than that their observation in the presence of persons of a different religious persuasion, even domestic servants,[3] made us shy, embarrassed and often restless.

It is universally assumed—by persons who have made education as a science the main object of their investigations—that mysticism in religion has a corrupting influence on the mind of a youth. They believe that the wellspring of ideas is thereby darkened at its source, feelings are confused and made impure, and insurmountable obstacles are laid in the way of the development of intellectual powers for one's entire lifetime. Thus they

---

3. [Eds.] Friedländer grew up in the prominent Jewish household of Moses Friedländer, prosperous silk merchant in Königsberg, who sent his son to establish the family business in Berlin. This text gives an autobiographical account of Friedländer's early experiences and struggles with his tradition.

urge that youth be protected from this. Nothing should be conveyed to young people but universally understandable statements expressed in clear and well-defined language—only conceptual elements that have the highest possible clarity even in the smallest details and are suited to the ability of the pupil to understand.

The observation is, on the whole, correct; centuries of experience among entire peoples confirmed it; and the educational principles based thereupon ought not be questioned by one of our inquirers into truth. But as experience incontrovertibly teaches, universal rules have their exceptions. The principle that youth is more easily taught and kept from error by communicating pure, clear, and easily understandable statements is manifestly overestimated and leads to another extreme. Especially in youth, the human soul needs a goal; it doubles its powers only through resistance and acquires higher degrees of perfection only through exertion, just as truth itself obtains its full interest only by means of the effort that it costs. The whole of life confirms for us that, whether in the moral or the physical realm, it is in our nature to learn to walk by blundering and falling.

It is true that secret narrations and mystical teachings, external customs and ceremonies bordering on the adventurous, all of which offer no meaning to the understanding, have in most cases the capacity to weaken the dynamism of the soul, to hem its ascent, and to form out of an intelligent person a slave, a mere *rational instrument,* as that worldly sage called a slave, a machine that can neither acquire nor deserve respect.[4] But it is no less true that what is widely considered a perverted education has had most fortunate consequences for individuals, especially among such persons who, as people of the first magnitude, have brilliantly affected the age in which they lived. These very assertions, which are not easily united with sound reason, and these empty customs, regarded as holy, have been the reason that these men have risen above their contemporaries.

Experience has seemed to confirm this phenomenon for us, to be sure, on a much smaller scale through a look at our own past.

---

4. [Eds.] An allusion to Aristotle's view in *Politics* 1.4 §1–5 that a slave is an "animate instrument," a form of household property that is intended for action and not for production.

The very turn of the soul to piety, feeling, and uplifting reverence at a young age; the very external customs that seem of great significance and do not characterize anything particular; that very element that stands out from the usual actions of life; the very harsh and alienating aspects of life that over time do not wholly diminish—these hold all the powers of a man's soul together in a bundle and do not allow them to be split up. Even uncultivated reason and memory burdened with little knowledge—when united with tender feeling and a reverential aversion to immorality, doubt, and frivolity—preserve the youthful mind from immorality and all-knowing arrogance; the inclination to scorn, and to seek out the ridiculous, which can easily be found in ceremonies, is thereby held in check; and that is no small gain. The ridiculous appears as contemptible, and the contemptible ceases to be the object of one's attention.

When the spark of reason ignites in the mind of a pious youth as he increases in age, so that understanding acquires predominance over the hazy impressionistic learning and enthused sensations, then in that case a powerful, thoughtful, morally complete, and, often, great man springs forth from the school of a much-decried mysticism. If this reasoning is well-founded and based on experience, one should probably expect that the phenomenon of being awakened by doubt and encouraged to become reflective would have to happen among our youth more often than among any others.

Reasons for awakening are greater and more pressing among them than among followers of other religions. In the first place, the teachings of the present system reigning among Jews, which run counter to common reason and are not to be equated with the teachings of their original religion, appear in less dubious light than does the mysticism of other religions. These teachings vacillate less than other religions between the limits of the comprehensible and the incomprehensible. Modern, ambiguous discourse has not required Jewish theologians to keep the harsh side of these matters as mild as possible and thus not insult the delicate eye of common sense. Supposing, however, that Jewish theologians had also felt this need; the nature of the Hebrew language is such that they could not satisfy it. A dead language does not readily acquire new concepts. Supposing, in addition, it were possible to alter arbitrarily Hebrew's literal sense; its peculiarly brilliant coloration would then shine through all concealment. This holds for all original languages that are now out of circulation and especially for Hebrew, which is such a figurative language.

A second reason why the young man of the Jewish religion is especially urged to give attention to these matters lies in the ceremonial laws. Their detailed prescriptions stand directly in our young man's way, for they are not applicable just to certain times and days, but they encompass the whole of one's life. From early morning until late night he either has to observe certain religious actions or take care not to transgress against something prescribed. The positive laws are embarrassing, burdened with costs, and wasteful of time; the negative ones set up barriers to his activity in our common life. Very often he comes into the uncomfortable situation of responding to his fellow creatures in an unsatisfactory manner. Nothing is more humiliating for a thoughtful person than this eternal condition of immaturity; instead of giving reasonable explanations for one's conduct, one always has to call upon the authorities of the law, especially if the matter concerns things that are trifling, i.e., the enjoyment of certain foods, a special style of clothing, and many other things whose number and triviality is equally great.

If, in spite of these inducements to become reflective, noble freethinkers are so few among us (we rightly exclude here those frivolous persons for whom the allures of the senses and bad influence lead to transgressions of ceremonial laws), the reason must lie in human moral nature. Even if this moral nature is capable of education, it requires, like lifeless nature, maintenance and care. If an insignificant and unremarkable circumstance can work against its development, how much more this is true of pressure, contempt, and worrying about sustenance. When these circumstances combine to affect a person, they reduce the entire capacity for thought to the mere preservation of the animal in a man and halt the growth of any other power. When, by contrast, happy circumstances conspire with genius and talent—to be sure, this occurs only rarely—then the intended effect is achieved, as happens when a Mendelssohn springs forth, unanticipated and much admired, from the nursery of mysticism and shapes himself into a model of practical wisdom.

If, in the words of this noble man,[5] it can be required that the
state shall consider and treat man as the *immortal son of the earth*
while religion is supposed to consider and treat him as *the image
of the creator*—a requirement that was partially realized in the
government of the great Friedrich[6]—the number of awakened
youths will increase more and more, and a certain spiritual formation will be anything but rare. A young man of the Jewish religion living in such a state during the bloom of his youth has not
had to share his parents' concerns for bread—a concern that cur-
tails all leisure—and his education invariably has been mystical;
entrance into the larger world, even among normally talented
youth, brings forth in him a marvelous reaction. His whole
sphere of thought suffers a beneficial shock: his desire for knowledge and contemplation are awakened, and sensations will follow this awakening, which, with ineffable attractions, invite one
to repeated striving.

Who can describe the passage from the slavery of the spirit into
freedom! Who can calculate the delight, and thus the strengthened energy of the soul, of a man who rises from the feeling that
he has shackles to the decision to throw them off! One ought not
to say that this ascent into culture is improbable and unbelievable.
No, in a state like Prussia everything has been prepared for that;
many-faceted harmonic, audible and pleasant tones awaken one
from a deep slumbering of the soul. The moderate constitution of
the government, the more elevated concepts of the age, a high-
mindedness that has become fine custom, the knowledge that is
spread through writings and schools—everything in such a constitutional state invites a neglected and otherwise suppressed
youth to a pleasant participation. Noble men affectionately
extend a hand to those who strive upward, point in friendship to
higher goals while encouraging such persons to reach their goals
through diligence. Instruction attained through such encouragement must necessarily teach one to appreciate, and in the end
make insignificant, that which is otherwise regarded as sacred.

Here's to the youth who does not throw out the whole kernel
with the husk! When the feeling of reverence for his religion, a

5. Whose principles and teachings we will continue to make our own. [Eds.:]
His footnote shows Friedländer's desire to be understood as Mendelssohn's heir.

6. [Eds.] Friedrich II (the Great), king of Prussia 1740–86.

feeling that he has nurtured in his soul from childhood on, turns away from the accidental, it turns all the more to that which is essential. When hatred of that which has caused him such great unpleasantness in civil conditions is outweighed by love for that which in the most important situations of life grasps us so deeply and indispensably! The mighty leap that his spirit must produce in order to work its way out of mystical confusion can all too easily cast him beyond truth and into the contrasting evil of doubt and unbelief. And this can occur more easily when the situation has been made more oppressive and embarrassing because the unshakable devotion of his forebears, strengthened through pressure, has plunged him into merely accidental externalities. The outlook of his mind is no longer unbiased and pure; all too easily it is clouded and rendered false by the weakness of an offended heart, so that truth, which was mixed in with mysticism, no longer appears to him in the form of truth.

A better lot, dear Sir, has befallen us, and we can do nothing other than bless the effect that the earlier paternal education has had on us in later years. In earlier times, when contact with foreign brothers in faith made us feel what was lacking in our first instruction, when that contact became the impetus for escaping the harnessing bonds of custom and putting trust into one's own searching, and when the external nature of our devotional practices, which do injury to sense and spirit, dawned upon us, it was solely that contact with men of noble morals and cultivated reason that still preserved us from the other, perhaps more corrupting, extreme of irreligion, and from the aimlessness of the customs so readily attached to it. In place of some contrary destiny, by which our youthful warmth of heart would have been more able to transform itself into an even deadlier coldness, this warmth—thanks be to providence!—has been preserved, but wholly related to the essentials of our religion, which we are no more able to dispense with than we are with our life.

Our innermost conviction tells us that we have described the path of our education according to the whole truth and that we have not been led, through vanity, to place ourselves in a more advantageous light. We did not begin to consider religion, duty, and vocation only yesterday. Without possessing actual scholarly knowledge, and being reared to a certain class that is common to the lot of our brothers—namely, the merchant class—we have had the leisure and the drive to direct our view away from the customary affairs of life and towards more important objects. According to our insights we have doubted, examined, and reproached, and finally taken sides. What we have chosen may still need many a correction and may be amenable to many additions. But the basis on which our system rests, the principles we have accepted and, as it were, incorporated into our intellectual nature, we feel are unshakable and indestructible—or our entire power of thought would have to undergo a profound overturning.

We do not hesitate to confess freely that a serious examination of the systems of religion generally and the teachings that lie behind the Mosaic in particular are occasioned by something other than the interest of pure truth. The political constitution of our brethren in almost every region of Europe has contributed not a little to it. The heavy burdens they bear everywhere; their exclusion from all branches of artistic endeavor and social activity; the prohibition of all property ownership and farming; and particularly the contempt under which they languish (sometimes less, sometimes more), which suppresses all courage: already at an early age all these burdens had to pain one's heart and embitter the mind. Upon a more calm consideration we could not conceal from ourselves that this almost universal treatment of our fellow men is not merely the one-sided result of Christian religious hatred and deeply rooted Christian prejudices. One needs no particularly deep insight to realize that much of that would also[7] have to be ascribed to our own not less deeply rooted prejudices, especially on account of our ceremonial law. The habits and customs that are partly intimidating and partly repellent; the separation the law requires that especially affects sociability; the impatience that has also taken root among the oppressed not less deeply than among their oppressors makes any reconciliation difficult or nearly impossible under such conditions. This situation had to lead us very naturally to an investigation of the Mosaic constitution, its spirit, its purpose and its applicability in our times, customs, climate, and form of government.

With the universal spread of the light of reason, with the liberal way of thinking of our contemporaries in the Protestant religion, and with the wise government of our land, which also

---

7. [Eds.] Reading *"auch"* for *"anch."* KGA I.2: 387, 20.

corresponds to this spirit, we were able and were permitted to engage and give voice to considerations that still slumber undeveloped in the souls of Jews and Christians of different times and places or that they had to suppress vigorously from fear of charges of heresy and persecution. In our day each religious group may determine as indisputably true that there is still middle ground between each positive religion and irreligion; that it doesn't necessarily follow that someone embraces the atheistic system just because he puts the faith of his church in doubt or is no longer able to accept a part of its teachings unconditionally. All participants in the sphere of the theological sciences of our time, all great teachers who stand at the pinnacle of the Protestant churches don't just admit to themselves but openly and courageously teach that the spirit, the core, the most essential aspect of all religions can, without exception, only consist of those truths that lead to the greatest happiness for the whole of mankind and to the greatest possible education, perfection, and development of all their powers. In other words, among wise persons it is no longer in dispute that our true knowledge of God and his infinite qualities, of our duties towards our fellow man, and of our definition as an immortal being that continues to exist in another world are the foundational pillars of our virtue and our happiness.

These forms of knowledge have never been the exclusive property of some one people. Rather, in all times and all places wise persons have developed these truths for themselves by exerting their power of reason and by attentively observing nature, which surrounds and speaks to them partly with the requisite clarity and conciseness and partly less clearly and coherently, but always in the tone and spirit of the age. The truths that these men have utilized as the foundation of their many-faceted systems also serve as the basis of our religion and moral teaching. We build on nothing else and can build on nothing else. The whole advantage that various teachers of religion ascribe to revelation over merely natural knowledge seems to us, if one looks at the matter with a critical eye, to consist of the following: religious teachers do not deny the divinity of human reason, this noblest gift of the all-goodness of God, but according to their view it is supposed to have been only a power dwelling in a finite creature not mighty enough to teach these truths, which are so indispensable for grounding the well-being of the human race with an appropriate intelligibility, authority, and dignity. What the tradition teaches us should thus conform perfectly to the wisdom and goodness of God: that these truths have been made known to man in an extraordinary manner. Thus the truths should become more urgent and their propagation occur faster and more universally; thus they should have gained as infinitely in inner effectiveness as a divine teacher is infinitely more sublime than a human teacher. Moreover, the dignity of the lawgiver should much better protect against mischievous wit and over-refined sagaciousness, against the ridicule of the former and the disturbing doubt of the latter.

For the moment we can leave untouched the variety of opinions about the manner in which these treasures are best acquired, and we can wish, rather, to dwell on an account of the same and on an enumeration of the individual principles. One may call these principles what one will: eternal truths, teachings of salvation, basic truths or yet some other, more clever names; whether they are further revealed to man through *nature* and through *things* or through *written* and *spoken signs,* honest inquirers of all parties always agree about the fact that they consist of the following principles:

1. *There is one God,* an uncreated, single, and simple essence, the creator, preserver, and judge of the world.

2. *The soul of man is immaterial,* a simple being distinguishable from matter. God has equipped it with immeasurable powers, which in accord with our powers of comprehension are capable of a growth that is not limited.

3. *The vocation of man here below is to strive for higher perfection and, hereby, the possession of happiness.* This happiness cannot be reached without goodwill and benevolence. The more man promotes order and harmony, cheerfulness and enjoyment, wisdom and virtue in the creation; that is to say, the more he spreads happiness, the happier he himself will be.

4. *The soul of man is immortal.* The human being is destined to continue in another condition when the body, as its present garment, disintegrates and decays. This expectation agrees with the nature of the creator and the essence of creatures blessed with reason. It harmonizes with the concept of an all-good and all-powerful God, and thus cannot possibly be false.

5. *God has created man for his, i.e., the human's, happiness.*[8] God has given man laws, i.e., God has bestowed power on man to recognize these rules to which human conduct must conform if man's welfare is to be promoted in the best manner. The least infraction of these rules does not go unnoticed and does not go without punishment. This punishment is a necessary and natural result of the action; thus it is not *revenge* of the creator; thus it is also not in relation to the majesty of the lawgiver, and thus it can also not last forever. It is a chastisement for improving the transgressor and must be desired by man himself, for it is indispensable and necessary for his perfection.

In our opinion these are the most important, greatest, and most consistent basic teachings that we need in order to recognize a higher determination of our nature, to be more inspired for the entirety of our duties, and to be strengthened for their courageous accomplishment.

We happily grant that the setting forth of these basic teachings needs polish and presumes to be neither the most precise nor best selected, and we are ready to accept any corrections of them with thanks. At the same time, we confess that insight into the reasons for these truths, however rightly and clearly they may be set forth, is too difficult for the great horde, for human beings taken as a whole; that, in addition, attentiveness and effort, thoughtfulness and skill in drawing conclusions are demanded, which only a few persons can accomplish; and that it is therefore most desirable to be able to strengthen (or, shall we say, replace) the inner reasons by external ones. We who consider ourselves inwardly convinced of the truth of these principles now return to the founder of our religion and direct our attention to the holy sources ascribed to him.

Here we find, according to the greatest historical certainty, that Moses already found pure precepts and concepts of religion, freed from all idolatry and superstition, as a worthy inheritance among the tribal elders of his nation. Above all, the tribal elders had sought to preserve the teaching of the existence of a spiritual deity who was not to be grasped through the senses. We find this teaching put forth in this purity by no other nation. But by the time of Moses the nomadic family had multiplied to become a

---

8. [Eds.] Italics not in text.

great people; and the lawgiver found this people sunken into the
oppression and misery of the most dire slavery among barbarians
and idolaters and rendered unreceptive to every truth. He freed it
from servitude, led it out of Egypt, and sought to shape it into an
independent nation. What an undertaking! It was only possible
for a man chosen by Providence when it needed an instrument
for the widest-ranging transformations, which extend their beneficial results to innumerable peoples over long centuries. History
knows few, if any, events with such impact as the dispersion of
this nation and its writings have had, and continue to have, on
humanity, from its rise to its decline, over thousands of years.

Following the path that Moses pursued to achieve his purpose,
we instantly recognize that he consulted the nature of man and
the character of the nation, as it was at that time, as if consulting
the holy oracles. But before we pursue the great lawgiver on his
path, we must describe his purpose in its full sublimity. As liberator of his people he wanted not only to lead them out of their
deep humiliation, not only to restore to them that sound and
authentic concept of God and his qualities—the holy property of
his ancestors; but he wanted also to make this people of *slaves*
into a people of *God*. His nation was supposed to preserve the
refined teaching of religion in its entire purity, to teach unceas-
ingly, and, as it were, to preach through its mere existence.

What an undertaking! Was it possible to carry out this sublime
plan with *this* people? The truths he wanted to teach the crude
horde are abstract and subtle; they require practice in contemplation, a developed understanding, and are usually only the fruit of
the leisure of a people that are at least protected against want,
enjoy peace, and have acquired independence. And his people
were a poor, merely sensual people, degraded by slavery, wan-
dering around in the desert without nourishment. In fact we also
see from history that Moses, right at the outset of his work, stumbled against an obstacle that constantly threatened his undertaking with demise. Even in the early days of lawgiving, since the
leader of the people was absent, the crude horde fell into the most
shocking idolatry and made an idol for itself and prayed to it. To
be sure, in his fiery zeal Moses destroyed the tablets of the law
and enacted strict regulations that had become necessary owing
to circumstances of the times, but his courage did not sink; he
pursued his plan and, instructed by this event, was led to a

method through which alone he was able to avoid missing his goal. He could not give his people pictures and pictorial writings, since these lead to superstition and idolatry, and his most prominent purpose was to preserve his people from just this. Nevertheless, the senses of such an outwardly sensuous people had to be engaged; at the level on which the people stood, they were not capable of any other manner of education. Thus Moses gave the people ceremonial law; this obligated them to actions; and the great maxim of the constitution was thus (in order to express ourselves briefly) to prescribe firmly only deeds and omissions, while merely inducing reflection. The people were to be driven to the former but only awakened to the latter.

The ceremonies were not supposed to hinder the knowledge of abstract truths but, rather, were to serve as a means of holding fast to those truths, to recall them and to cause devotion to them. If their suitability as a means to this purpose ceased to apply, they had to be dispensed with or changed, according to circumstances. And Moses, along with those animated with his spirit and his way of thinking, proceeded in accord with this maxim, as must be obvious to every unbiased inquirer. In Moses' system, God did not appear as creator and preserver of the universe but as the protector and covenanted friend of the nation and, finally, as its liberator, leader, and founder of its independence. State and religion were not separate, but one; not connected, but still the same. Thus everything in this constitution was surrounded with a strand of religious light: every civic service was an act of worship. The people were, and came to be called, God's people, God's property; their affairs were God's affairs, their contributions God's possessions, and even the lowliest battle-facility[9] was involved in worship. The same aura hovered around the ceremonial laws. They were the husk in which the great teaching of religion, the actual kernel, lay concealed.

In light of the lawgiver's wisdom we can assume, even though this cannot be proved in every single instance, that each custom and each commandment had its authentic meaning that went hand in hand with the welfare of the nation and its moral stature. From those commandments whose purpose has been stated or is

---

9. [Eds.] Friedländer cites Deuteronomy 23:13 ff., which makes a veiled reference to regulations for a field privy.

clearly discernible to the eye, it is reasonable to infer which of the other commandments are likely to appear to us as purposeless, petty, or even entirely ridiculous. Even the members of society who had to fulfill the commandments were not aware (or, at least, not clearly aware) of their purpose; it was sufficient for the law-giver if, for the moment, the fulfillment of the commandments contributed something to their general or individual happiness. To anyone who inquired, however, they gave cause for reflection or an occasion for instruction by the sages and popular leaders.

The very spirit of the entire system clearly demonstrates that this hypothesis is not invented in order to save these laws. The written laws were few, and even these were, for the most part, unintelligible without oral commentary. It was axiomatic that it was forbidden to write down anything concerning the laws. It was even explicitly stated, "Teachings intended for oral instruction you must not entrust to writing."[10] The unwritten laws were thus taught only through oral transmission; and for reasons just as understandable as judicious, these laws remained vague.

The teacher of the people in every generation was thereby given a free hand to alter and to adapt the commandments according to the conditions of the time. No one, with the book of laws in hand, could contradict the teacher, for in this respect there were no written laws. "Even though this school affirms what that school denies"—it is explicitly stated concerning the ceremonial laws—"both utterances still express the word of the living God."[11] This statement and many others in the Talmud demonstrate incontestably that according to the plan of the first law-giver the sages of each generation would retain a free hand to expand or limit the laws linked to time and place to give them a more precise interpretation or to cancel them completely, all according to the needs of the time and to the moral customs and the general progress of the nation.[12]

10. *Babylonian Talmud*, Giffin 60b, Tenurah 14b.

11. *Babylonian Talmud*, Eruvin 13b.

12. [Eds.] Friedländer quotes from Deuteronomy 17: 8–11: "If a legal case is too baffling for you to decide, be it a controversy over homicide, civil law, or assault—or any other matter which happens inside your gates—you shall promptly repair to the place that the Lord your God will have chosen, and appear before the Levit-ical priests, or the magistrate in charge at the time, and present your problem. When they have announced to you the verdict in the case, you shall carry out the

Not only is this cancellation of the laws linked to time and place grounded in the nature of the constitution and evident throughout all of sacred scripture, but in addition the teachers[13] of the people, who came much later, from whom the respect, spirit and authority of the first lawgiver had long since been withdrawn, also acknowledged the cancellation as fundamental. How else could these teachers have canceled or on their own authority altered many laws, the observance of which in foreign lands and in different climates had no application or was subjected to great difficulties?[14]

Not until even less fortunate times, after service in the temple and constitution were destroyed and the dispersed nation sank into unprecedented misfortune, did the remaining teachers of law, driven by necessity, as they themselves confessed, make the desperate extra-legal decision: to entrust those laws that had been preserved through oral transmission to writing and thus give them lasting permanence. They themselves named this action, using a verse of the Psalms,[15] "the destruction of the law."[16] And that, rightly so. As soon as the ceremonial actions, as signs, no longer call to mind what they designated, as soon as the

---

verdict that is announced to you from that place that the Lord chose, observing scrupulously all their instructions to you. You shall act in accordance with the instructions given you and the ruling handed down to you; you must not deviate from the verdict that they announce to you either to the right or to the left," here cited in *Tanakh: The Holy Scriptures* (Philadelphia/Jerusalem: Jewish Publication Society, 1985). He then adds, "Sziphri comments that 'right nor left' means: Even when it appears to you that a teacher on the right says left, and a teacher on the left says right, do not deviate and follow." See *Sifre: A Tannaitic Commentary on the Book of Deuteronomy*, tr. Reuven Hammer, Yale Judaica Series, vol. 24 (New Haven and London: Yale University Press, 1986).

13. [Eds.] Reading *"Lehrer"* for *"Lehren."* KGA, 1.2, 393, 3.

14. Here especially belongs: the *Levirate marriage*, which was even forbidden although it was required positively and without limitation; the laws of inheritance and of the first-born; and laws concerning usury, all of which have undergone considerable changes.

15. Psalms 119:126.

16. It is a time when one must destroy the law for the sake of the eternal will. [Eds.:] In his anti-Halachic polemic, Friedländer appears to have inverted and then paraphrased the meaning of this verse from Psalm 119, a Psalm in praise of Torah. Compare the Revised Standard Version of Ps. 119:126: "It is time for the Lord to act, for thy law has been broken."

practices have no authentic meaning and occasion no convictions
that lead to moral and social activity, everything degenerates into
works righteousness, into idle talk and empty trivialities. The
practices are the body, whose spirit is the doctrine. If the soul has
fled, of what use any longer is the stripped-off husk? The butter-
fly has escaped; the empty cocoon lies there. This, we believe, is
true of all ceremonies in the world, both religious and civil, both
in earlier times and in our own days.

One's glance lowers in sadness and defeat at the history of the
Jews, who have ceased to be, and to be called, a nation. With sympathetic melancholy one wanders among the ruins of their temple and their state constitution,[17] which in the times of their
flowering were so tightly bound together, so completely pieces of
a single whole. It has happened with the Jews as it had to happen: even in their very disfiguration we recognize the eternal
laws of nature and of the human spirit. Imagination, full of sad
images of earlier times, and unbridled inclinations—that so easily
obtain preponderance over cool reflection and calm reasoning
among the dispersed nation, which was without any direction
and independence—soon were bound to gain the upper hand.
Superstition and wanton enthusiasm were bound to dominate,
first only to cloud the original pure religion, then wholly to con-
taminate it.

Such a people, sunken into misery and inferiority, will soon fill
out their lack of knowledge of the invisible with absurdities. In
place of true virtue, whose essence consists in an eternal struggle
with our desires and passions, practices and formalities will step
in that are tedious in the extreme and that have as their object the
mere castigation of the body. With the sagacity inbred in it, this
people will brood over its sacred scriptures, which neither time
nor barbarian hand have been able to destroy. Amid these ruins,
which even artists would secretly have to admire, this destitute,
unfortunate people, driven by time and destiny, seeks, and imagines it has found, a place of refuge. Without a feeling for the
beauty of the whole, without taste for harmony and unanimity,

17. [Eds.] Cf. the description of traditional Judaism in this section of the *Open
Letter* with Schleiermacher's description of Judaism in Speech V in his *On Reli-
gion: Speeches to Its Cultured Despisers*, Richard Crouter, ed. and tr. (Cambridge:
Cambridge University Press, 1996).

its imagination will wander and gaze in astonishment at the defective brick that has lost its color; it will find much to admire in the play of nature that has produced an ugly vein in the marble. The idea of erecting a new, livable building out of these fragments does not occur to such a people; they take enjoyment in rubble and grass.

All of this has happened to the greatest degree among the Jews. As the ceremonial law became inapplicable and as it degenerated into empty actions, so the basic truths were also obscured for them. In vain did the prophets of earlier times, wholly in the spirit of Moses, rail against the purposelessness of these ceremonial laws and insist upon the pursuit of the social virtues. These men, who had great diversity but shared an equally high purpose, strove in vain to give a more spiritual direction to a sensual religion that degenerated more and more into works righteousness; they did this to prepare human understanding for a more spiritual religion, if this ever can be the lot of finite creatures. Their efforts were of no avail, and even Isaiah, the greatest speaker among the prophets, only squandered his rhetorical skill against the purposelessness of bodily chastisements; in vain he recommended the observance of social duties as the only and most worthy worship, even under threat of divine punishment. In his own words, "the heart of this people was hardened, the ear deafened, the eye blinded, so that it neither sees nor hears, nor contemplates from the heart, nor repenting, turns and heals."[18]

But the condition became more unfortunate by far in still later times. Dispersed throughout the world and completely abandoned, with no permanent abode, no civil sovereign, and no spiritual leader, the people finally lost all touch with the values of reason and all inclination for the higher truths that had made up the foundation of their original religion. Instead, they fulfilled the ceremonial laws with scrupulous exactitude. The beautiful edifice of their religion was destroyed, and those who escaped the collapse embraced the ruins not of the temple but of its scaffolding—that is, the external customs—the only thing they had rescued. Had their spirit not been so profoundly crushed and their

18. Isa. 6:10: "Dull that people's mind, stop its ears, and seal its eyes—Lest seeing with its eyes, and hearing with its ears, it also grasp with its mind, and repent and heal itself." *Tanakh* (JPS, 1985).

psychic powers so paralyzed, they would have learned, in other lands and under other conditions, to give up the ceremonial laws as something that had become completely useless. Yet because of their state of mind at the time, their adherence to these laws grew increasingly stronger; the greater the persecutions became, the more anxiously their teachers, who lacked spiritual inspiration, urged the fulfillment of meaningless actions.

To all this was added the idea of a messiah, which completely clouded their minds and made all independent perspective impossible. This idea arose quite early, as a result of the mistaken interpretation of passages containing the inspired words of their prophets. In all these prophetic utterances the messiah, or the redeemer from prevailing hardship and distress, appeared as the customary figure of consolation. If the people repented of their sins—so proclaimed the prophets in all their oracles—they were supposed to be freed of the yoke of oppression and returned to the land of their fathers. This idea became ever more deeply rooted. The more the likelihood decreased that redemption would take place by natural means, the more the hope grew stronger for a return to Jerusalem by miraculous means. If the people of God were to dwell once again in the land of their fathers, their return had to be bound to the restoration of the ancient political order, to service in the temple and to sacrifices. This delusion was much beloved by the people and was entirely in keeping with the spirit of the slogans of their seers and demagogues, who in their vision of the future could not imagine—because of the situation at the time—the liberation of their nation by any other means.

Accordingly, they had to accept the strict fulfillment of the ceremonial laws as indispensable for two reasons: first, in order to be worthy of the miraculous redemption through these meritorious acts; and second, in order to be able, upon arriving in Jerusalem, to live according to the ancient political order and to fulfill the will of God. This expectation of the messiah and the return to the promised land had to fortify the inclination to direct all efforts and all contemplation to ancient history, to service in the temple and sacrifice, to ceremonial laws. All faculties of the soul were devoted to these studies; all ingenuity was focused on hairsplitting musings. Their scholars multiplied, perverted, made the already burdensome ceremonial laws more difficult and thus increased the separation of the Jews from other peoples and from other subjects of human knowledge.

The more meticulous the ceremonial laws became and the more creditable they were, the more the people's demand for speedy redemption, for miraculous deliverance from misfortune. They overworked their brains and those of their contemporaries with responses to hairsplitting questions concerning observance of the laws that would come into effect should they return to Jerusalem, or with the solution of the most trifling problems, all of which inclined to childishness and eccentricity. Given this frame of mind, it is easy to perceive not only how the under-standing and—most likely—the moral customs of the people were increasingly corrupted but also how even their external appearance must have taken on a one-sidedness bordering on caricature. Accompanying this was an ever more rapidly increas-ing ignorance of their original language. That which was known through exegesis, together with the scarcely comprehensible translations, contributed to the dissemination of even more erro-neous concepts. Moreover, the power of imagination, which in any case had been unbridled, was provided with a new opportu-nity to generate fantastic notions and extravagant expectations. Under the circumstances in which the people found themselves, it was hardly to be expected that the teachers would suspend those ceremonial laws that had become inapplicable and replace them with other laws better suited to the spirit of the times. It was even less likely that these leaders, who were no longer capa-ble of spiritual elevation and who had a scant knowledge of Hebrew, could extract the universal religious concepts and moral teachings expounded in sacred scripture, order them systemati-cally, and present them to the best of their ability—even, if need be, in the adulterated language of the people—for the enlighten-ment and moral edification of the people.

What finally had to strengthen and turn the longing for Jerusa-lem and the hope for the messiah into the most fervent wish of the people was the fact that this longing and this wish were trans-posed into the liturgy, thereby becoming an integral part of the worship of God and of prayer. In its original constitution Judaism had neither formulas for prayer nor devotional practices. Animal and other sacrifices took their places. With the destruction of the state, and as the Jews became scattered among other peoples, this void had to be filled and a different service of worship arranged. The formulas of prayer, which were now composed—partly from individual verses of sacred scripture, partly of one's own invention (yet their style betrayed the weaknesses of an aging language)—intoned the eternally recurring laments about the misery oppressing the nation, the sighs about returning to the lost land, the longing for the restoration of the temple cult.

In all these prayers, without exception—indeed, even in the thanksgiving for food, in the words of blessing under the marriage tent—the lamentation of slaves yearning for salvation rang out, the prayer for a messiah who would lead the dispersed remnant of Israel back to Palestine. From century to century these prayers became worse and more numerous, the ideas more mystical and tainted by the principles of the Kabbalah, which downright contradicted the authentic spirit of Judaism. Finally, the language in which they were expressed not only offends the ear but also ridicules all logic and grammar. The greatest portion of the nation understands nothing of these prayers; and this is no small good fortune, since in this way they produce no effect, either for good or ill, on the mind of those praying.

In a brief sketch, this is the history of the external religion of our people in past centuries. I need not remind you, esteemed Sir, that the circumstances of the Christian church in those barbarous times were scarcely any better. A deep darkness had taken possession of all thinking, and human reason succumbed to the yoke of superstition and wanton enthusiasm. For centuries one traverses what were desolate regions for true virtue and morality; crude customs and unbridled passions rule, and no seed of humanity has yet to sprout up. True scholarship has disappeared; in its place a brooding scholasticism has emerged, which occupies the mind with investigations of objects that now scarcely seem believable to us. Textbooks, public speeches, and church prayers all bear the stamp of a crippled understanding that arouses deep pity, of a corrupted common sense that arouses horror. With the annals of humanity in hand we could, I think, dare to say that Christianity in those times had sunk even deeper than the religion of the Jews. Finally, after a long night, yet slowly with irresistible force, a day of better insight dawned, and with it the feelings and sensations for the good and the beautiful became ennobled.

Since the Reformation, Protestant Christianity has taken giant steps, even though our brethren, held back by a thousand hindrances, could not follow them. But changes in the moral world have a remarkable analogy with changes in the physical world. Just as the extermination of wild animals, the clearing of primal forests, and the reclamation of foul marshes not only have their beneficial effect on what lies immediately adjacent but also spread health and life and prosperity into further regions, so the progress of the Christian church has a beneficial effect on the Jews. Since one no longer persecutes them with fire and the sword, since one now and then allows them to raise their head; in a word, since a feeling of honor and, with it, social inclinations are awakened in them, they have come closer to Christians in convictions and mental perfection.

And thus as governments have become more moderate and more well meaning towards the Jews, beams of light that the churches give forth dissipate the fog in the synagogue. Just as enlightened Christians have learned to appreciate Catholic and other practices, so the better minds and whole better families among the Jews do with respect to the ceremonial and ritual law: Everything that draws attention away from what is essential in religion, that suppresses understanding, and that harms true morality is not merely indifferent for a thoughtful person of any religious party but is, depending on the effect of these influences, quite repugnant. If our fellow men, the Christians, have the advantage of universally developed institutions of learning, an infinitely better civil constitution, and religious practices that do not reach so deeply into everyday life as the ceremonial laws, so for their part our brethren, the Jews, have the advantage, which compensates for the lack of former advantages, that they do not need to subject the dogmas of their religion to some purifying fiery examination.

Let us explain ourselves more precisely. We have confessed with candor that the practices that are so trivial and go into tiniest detail no longer have any value for us; that they are not just indifferent to us but also, for this reason, must therefore become repugnant because the ruminating and brooding about them wreaks havoc on the higher, more essential purposes of religion. But apart from the error of their being insignificant and costing time and energy, they do, as a consequence, no further immediate harm to practical morality. Much greater is the effect of supersensible dogmas that, apart from the fact that they denigrate reason, also directly assault morality. Falsified doctrinal teachings are infinitely more damaging to the human spirit than ceremonies that are merely strange. The absolutely false teaching about fatalism, which, to be sure, is not found in Christianity, attacks the inner aspect of ethics and undermines its foundation. Such teachings poison the source of the convictions from which, alone, moral actions flow.

If the better Jew merely needs to shed the husk of his ceremonial laws in order to purify religion, the better Christian must subject his basic truths to a new examination, something demanding far more effort and thought. If, despite this considerable advantage, it is not to be denied that at least with respect to their numbers the education of Jews is far behind that of Christians, this is obviously related to their political conditions. Nevertheless, time and circumstance have caused a profitable exchange of ideas between both related religions. These religions, which moral customs and ideas had for centuries held as far apart from each other as the seas and mountains divide one people from another, have drawn closer to one another in a remarkable fashion. The Jews' greatest gain no doubt lies in the fact that the longing for the messiah and for Jerusalem has departed ever further from their hearts as reason has increasingly rejected these expectations as chimerical. It is always possible that single individuals, confined to their quarters or in other respects removed from worldly affairs, still entertain such wishes within their souls. Yet among the majority of Jews, at least those in Germany, Holland, and France, this notion receives no support and the last traces of it will ultimately be eradicated.

As Jews have drawn nearer to Christians a second great advantage for the former has arisen through their well-known need to care for the moral and rational instruction of their children. And although we also admit here, with our usual directness, that the moral textbooks produced by its members, in Hebrew, for this purpose are partly incomplete and, on account of increasing ignorance of the ancient language, partly unusable;

still it is no less true that these very textbooks are becoming ever more superfluous.[19] The German language obtains ever more of a place in our midst, and a most excellent instruction of youth can be conducted from German textbooks.[20]

What can hinder our future scholars from following the Christians' example of seeking out the sources of moral teaching in the original documents themselves and making these usable for our progeny? You, dear Sir, know well that the law book of Moses, the holy poets and prophets, and many fragments from the Talmud—and especially from Maimonides, who created his whole system of ethics from Aristotle—contain a great wealth of seeds from which a sense of virtue and feeling of duty can be developed.

With regard to education, we have said that despite many advantages and at least as regards their numbers the Jews were far behind the Christians, and we are happy to repeat this admission. Our brothers, the Christians of the Protestant religion, have hurried on far ahead of us, and in the near future we shall have great trouble catching up with them. But this holds true only for the development of intellectual powers—for the acquisition of knowledge—not for morality. In view of this we must rather give witness to the fact that our brothers do not stand one rung lower on the ladder of moral worth than any other learned, refined, and cultivated people.

This declaration will get attention, and we expect loud protest. Not from you, worthy Sir—who, exalted above all selfishness, does full justice to us, and at least will allow no derogatory opinion against an oppressed nation, and does so all the less, since

19. [Eds.] As a patron of the *Haskalah* in Berlin, Friedländer was a cofounder of the first modern Jewish school, the Jüdische Freischule. See Steven M. Lowenstein, *The Jewishness of David Friedländer and the Crisis of Berlin Jewry* (Ramat-Gan, Israel: Bar-Ilan University, 1994), 8. Later, as a leader of the community, Friedländer also wrote a Hebrew textbook for the use of school children.

20. Only for prayers and devotional exercises is nothing available up to now. These still consist of an empty babbling that can neither elevate nor bring forth holy experiences in a well-ordered mind. And nothing can be done about this, short of undertaking a total reform with the Jews, even in civil matters. Instruction and education of youth is an affair of private persons; changes in worship belong to the whole community, for which partly a more common spirit and partly more agreement of minds are needed.

you already know how important such an opinion is and how devastating it would be for these unfortunate persons—but probably from the side of the great gossiping horde, which takes no end of enjoyment in such derogatory remarks that greatly flatter one's ego. The Jews simply have the reputation of great immorality, and it is no small risk to go against the general opinion about this matter, especially since, in more recent times, men who daily mount their philosophical lectern have not been ashamed to issue cutting judgments without any evidence.[21]

Yet before one accuses us of crude partisanship, listen to us and then contradict us, if one can, through facts and reasons.

It is truly not so easy to pass judgment about the worth of an entire people; and it becomes even less easy the more this people is distinctive in customs, practices, and conditions. Without being clearly conscious of it, every religious group takes its church to be the one that alone brings blessings, and thus it believes that mankind can only receive the highest moral education in its school. When raised in a different greenhouse, the noblest product of humanity appears immature, full of deficiencies, and incomplete. At the very least it thinks that things would turn out better if everyone had been raised on its soil.

Only history and experience can recognize these fallacies and teach how to rectify the judgments. If one proceeds with these signposts and observations, it will follow that if the whole human race really makes continual progress in the instruction of its intellectual and moral powers, this progress is communicated commensurately and becomes noticeable in the individual body, in each smaller group that makes up the larger society. The same

21. [Eds.] Compare, for example, Kant's lectures from 1798, *Anthropology from a Pragmatic Point of View*, tr. Victor Lyle Dowdell and ed. Hans H. Rudnick (Carbondale & Edwardsville: Southern Illinois University Press, 1978), 101, footnote *: "The Palestinians, living among us, or at least the greatest number of them, have through their usurious spirit since their exile received the not-unfounded reputation of deceivers. It seems strange to think of a nation of deceivers; but it is just as strange to think of a nation made up of nothing but merchants, which are united for the most part by an old superstition that is recognized by the government under which they live. They do not seek any civil honor, but rather wish to compensate their loss by profitably outwitting the very people among whom they find protection, and even to make profit from their own kind. It cannot be otherwise with a whole nation of merchants, who are nonproductive members of society (for example, the Jews in Poland)."

degree of religion and irreligion, of virtue and vice, is proportionately shared by everyone, assuming that a certain class of people is not treated like the Helots in antiquity or the Negroes in our times. If the inhabitants of a certain state generally have acquired a decisive advantage over the inhabitants of some other one, this is certainly attributable to the fact that the Jews of this state have also distinguished themselves in an exemplary manner.

Generally, morality is far less the result of instruction than the fruit of social intercourse, than the example of a parental home, of affiliations, and, in later years, of one's business dealings. A human being carries the capacity for this in his moral feelings; instruction provides a far weaker impulse toward cultivation of this capacity than example, and one's own continued practice brings the precious fruit to greater maturity.

"You," we might call out to those who absolutely wish to burden us with an innate wickedness; "You, who intend to humble us simply by shouting: Jew. We feel the whole weight of the contempt that you press together in these two tiny syllables.[22] But if you really pay homage to the truth and to humanity, as you allege, show us a more religious people in whom the virtues of humanity are more often encountered than among us. Which people practices true benevolence to a higher degree, which does not bother to inquire about someone's ecclesiastical faith or nationality? Where is fatherly and child-like love, where the sacredness of marriage more deeply rooted? Where are self-sacrifices for the good of others more frequent or greater? Where is there a more moral people among whom the brutal crimes of murder, robbery, deadly assault, and treason are more rare? Among whom are unnatural vices and depraved moral customs less frequent?

"We expect a response to these questions if our testimony is to be refuted. With declamations and with appeals to the authority of the enemies of Jews of the previous century—or even of the present one—indeed with all your proofs of documentation of crimes in foreign lands where Jews are treated with an unspeakable harshness, you do not contradict the experience in our regions; you do not sap the claims of reason and truth. Only do

22. [Eds.] *Ju-de.*

not single out certain crimes high-handedly,[23] do not arbitrarily
ink the stamp of repudiation, which you therefore press on certain faults because they especially adhere to the Jews, who
engage exclusively in a special kind of business. You reproach
them for *bribery, betrayal,* and *usury* as their characteristic vices.
But who has given you the right to cast a contemptuous glance at
a *bribing Jew,* while closing one's eye to the *bribed judge?* Actually,
who has given you the right to classify the errors and vices of
men and to declare betrayal and usury to be the first, most shocking vices that subvert the state? Indeed, ponder a bit before you
summarily condemn, that it cannot have anything to do with the
religion of Jews if they are especially subject to these vices.

"Your lawgiver, who wanted to hold them back from all social
intercourse with other peoples, who absolutely wanted to turn
them into farmers, not merchants, forbade them all interest,
including even that which is legal according to our laws of the
land; and nevertheless those in this religious confession, just
because they are Jews, must they by all means be deceivers and
usurers? Oh, indeed, surrender to truth, which offers itself so
easily, and recognize that it is merely in the excluding occupation—to which the ruling party has condemned the Jews—in
commerce, where they make themselves guilty of the faults of
deception and of taking all sorts of advantages more than any
other classes of citizens. And if that does not suffice for you, then
go and inquire into the character of other small merchants and
second-hand dealers—your business-pursuing fellow Christians, who do not stand under immediate police purview and
who at the same time engage in trade with the products of their
diligence—enumerate and calculate *their* deceit and *their* misdeeds; consider these according to their gravity and number,
together with the deceitful misdeeds of Jews, and be—unbrib-
able judges."

23. We do not know the Jews in Italy well enough. But the Jews in Livorno certainly have a different education from the Jews in Rome; and in both places they
are judged according to the worth of their fellow subjects. It is certain that among
Jews in Italy there are no assassinations at all. This derives from the fact—as the
armchair psychologists say—that all Jews are cowardly. To which one can add:
and because the asylum of the [Roman Catholic] church is not available to them.
But might one then seriously wish them a braveness that is required for stabbing
someone in the back?

Forgive, most worthy Sir, this unintended digression, which we have considered necessary to save the honor of our religious brethren. We do not wish to protect the rabble among Jews; yet we require that one distinguish Jewish rabble from Jews in the same way that one distinguishes Christian rabble from Christians.

We return now to our subject. Even if, according to our exposition, the ceremonial laws exercise neither a useful nor a harmful influence on morality or on the *duties of man,* we do not thus hesitate to confess that they might hinder us in exercising the *duties of a citizen*—if these were to be demanded of us. Experience in modern times has, to be sure, proved that our brethren have also fulfilled these duties with courage. Yet either these members have in some states been forcibly coerced into civil obedience in an unspeakably horrible manner; or in places where taking on these duties has really happened out of free choice, as long as the ceremonial laws are not formally abolished, those who transgress them are still always suspected of frivolous behavior, the spread of which is hardly desirable. I am convinced that abolishing these laws under present conditions is much in accord with the spirit of the Mosaic system and is not only desirable for our own relief but is also necessary in order to make it possible for us to fulfill the duties of a citizen.

The duty of *self-preservation* and *preservation of the descendants* is, as we think, a no less important motivation. We are convinced that it is the indispensable duty of every man to promote his external condition or his well-being (which more or less stands in relation to the ennobling of the inner man) on the path of virtue and honesty. Similarly holy is one's duty to place the descendants in a position where, through the cultivation of their talents and capabilities, they not only are able to become useful in the larger public society but also become able to take part in the higher happiness of a more cheerful enjoyment of life. This is impossible in the present situation of the nation, which is still more or less limited on all sides and cannot determine itself in accord with free choice and the urging of its inclinations. Taken together, all these reasons insist, with united strength, on casting off the burdensome yoke of ceremonial and ritual laws, whose abolition the lawgiver himself would teach and enjoin if he lived in our times.

But why, one might ask, if the authority of the lawgiver and one's own discernment, wisdom, and duty, if the innermost

conviction of the rightness of the action all point toward a single
aim, namely, toward the cancellation of the ceremonial laws,
then why do you procrastinate? Why do you hesitate to declare
that these laws are no longer binding on you, that you are ready
to abandon the religion of your fathers (insofar as it is understood as the fulfillment of these laws and customs) and—to convert to Christianity? Here, worthy friend of virtue, our startled
conscience bids us pause. Here we face the abyss, which we
know neither how to circumvent nor how to leap over. In short,
here is the point at which we seek your counsel, your assistance,
and your instruction.

With the same audacious candor with which we have presented the results of our investigations concerning the law of
Moses and the foundations of the Mosaic religion, and with the
same love of truth, we must confess that which is surely sufficiently clear from our presentation, namely, to abandon the religion of our fathers, i.e., the ceremonial laws, and to accept the
Christian religion are to us two entirely different matters.

Of course, we have before us the example of a great number of
members of our nation. In all times and all lands there have been
persons who, without external force, have voluntarily left their
religion, or what they took it to be, and gone over to Christianity,
be it a Catholic or a Protestant side. We do not intend to judge
them. Where inclinations and feelings unintentionally mix into
the office of judgment, cold reason as the sole appropriate judge
seldom reaches a pure and wholly unbiased judgment. It is
always possible that those persons have taken, with thoughtfulness and with conviction about the truth of the new religious
principles, what appears to us to be a rash step. The rupture of all
family ties, the giving up of all duties to the old religious society
may appear shocking to us, but to them the sacrifice that they
brought to their conviction seemed a heroically worthwhile deed.
It is also always possible that these men have stifled the upset
feeling through overly fine rationalizations: human wit does not
have to look further for reasons, if an overwhelming advantage
attracts one to a deed. Finally, it is possible that they have merely
followed the urges of self-interest, which among common persons speaks much too loudly to be overruled by the voice of conscience. As we stated, we do not wish to judge these men, but
they also cannot serve us as exemplars or models.

It is not reputation that frightens us away from following their example. This reason is too paltry to be given much account in affairs of this importance. Also we do not fear the hate and persecution of our brothers, from whom we would thus forcibly withdraw. If we would continue to render friendship and service and to retain our dignity as virtuous persons—the bonds of family shall certainly remain eternally holy in our hearts—then hate would gain no roots, and the laws of the land would protect us against persecutions based on this change of religion, even if these were in the spirit of the times; then love and respect of the newly acquired religious brethren would have to compensate us for the lost love and respect of the former ones.

No, honorable Sir, we openly confess that if it could happen without compromising our reason and wounding our moral feeling, we would spare no consideration and publicly incorporate ourselves into the society that constantly holds open the portals of its temple and with equally open arms and friendly human hearts is always ready to receive us.

Yet there is more. We have striven to make clear to the best of our ability what we take to be the foundation of every religion and especially the religion of Moses. The individual principles of which this religion consists have, for us, the highest certainty; and we do not doubt that the Christian teacher to whom we would make a public confession of them—not as an aggregate of truths that we *believe* but about which we are *convinced*—would accept it, if not literally, as *identical* with the church's confession of faith, yet *agreeing* in spirit with this confession. From this angle, therefore, no difficulty would be found, and we would not fear that we would be rejected. But these principles are not all that we would bring with us from Judaism; in addition, we would bring along other principles of the utmost significance, whose truth is no less evident to us and which we are forced to accept out of conviction. Will these principles also conform to the teachings of the religious society that we are choosing? Will a teacher of the Christian Church be prepared if not to accept these principles then at least to tolerate them, allowing us publicly to confess these other principles which *for us* are matters of conviction and beyond doubt? We do not venture to answer this question in the affirmative; at the very least we must not make a decision regarding this without the consent of a teacher of religion as respected, learned, and noble as you, worthy Sir.

We are so bold as to lay before your teaching office these principles that we hold to be so essential and not without reason flatter ourselves that they will receive your approval. When we, sparked by a thirst for knowledge in the soul, set out to reflect upon truth and, according to our intellectual capacity, to recognize it by certain characteristics, we discovered, according to the guidance of those philosophers who deal more with practical knowledge than with speculative musings, the essential distinction between *truths of reason* and *truths of history,* which readily presents itself to common sense. *Truths of reason* can be accepted only through *conviction; truths of history,* only on *faith.* Truths of reason are based either on unchangeable relations and essential connections between concepts, by virtue of which they either presuppose or exclude each other, or on observations of unchangeable natural laws, which the wise will of the creator of the material world prescribed. Truths of this sort are capable of a higher degree of conviction than mere historical truths; but for those persons who wish to attain these truths it is indispensable that they seek for themselves, through their own thought and observation. Even if something had long been discovered by someone else, they rediscover it, as it were, for themselves. It is generally known that learning can create nothing new in the mind; it can only direct one's attention, avoid misconceptions, illuminate obscurities—in brief, at least facilitate the effort of one's own thought, which is impossible to dispense with, while ridding the path to truth of difficulties and smoothing it out. To require acceptance of these truths on authority is nonsense; anyone who wished to accept them thusly would not have the truths themselves but only *words;* such truths belong not to the memory but to reason and thus are intended to be grasped not by the former but by the latter.

By contrast, truths of history allow no testing of one's own, only comparison and evaluation of witnesses who handed them down to us; we can associate them with the series of truths known to us in no other way than on authority or through faith. To demand proof on rational grounds or evidence of one's own senses would in this instance be just as absurd as to require blind faith apart from one's own thinking and observing for eternal truths of reason or for unchangeable laws of nature. Yet even here authority and faith cease to apply at the moment that contradictions come to light—contradictions either in the data of history itself, which are impossible to reconcile, or in those higher truths, the conviction of which can in no wise be shaken in a rational soul. Certainty about the latter is unshakable; by contrast, this is not so in the case of the truths of history, and when a controversy thus arises it is just as impossible for the former to lose as it is necessary for the latter.

It is the case that truths of history can be *unusual;* this does not by itself destroy their credibility. Not everything that at first appearance looks like a contradiction and not everything that in the initial hasty view of history seems impossible to us must we reject as a fable or mere invention. Many a contradiction disappears with more precise investigation; many a seeming impossibility at bottom is merely not probable, merely not a daily event, merely fails to harmonize with the usual cycle of our ideas. Especially when dealing with early history, ancient authors use language that often induces us to hasty conclusions and judgments against which we have to be on guard. The magnificent inestimable property—which alone is characteristic of man—the gift of language, cannot deny its human origin. Whether they owe their origin wholly or only in part to the world of the senses, our concepts still take all of their designations from the sensual world. The signs of concepts can thus more or less become a source of deception and confusion. This holds for all languages without exception. Yet even when with a rising level of culture the wise persons of each age elevate above colloquial speech those expressions that designate immaterial concepts and withdraw them from everyday circulation, this means of preventing possible misinterpretation can still only occur among living languages, not among dead ones, and least of all with Hebrew, whose signs in and of themselves are so pictorial, and which is so abundant in tropes and figures.

Permit us, worthy friend of truth—since this open letter, if you approve it, might well become publicly known—to linger here more extensively, for the benefit of other readers, regarding the nature of the original language in which the sources are composed. Not only does the Hebrew language, with regard to its entire structure, i. e., in view of the regularity of its grammar, carry in itself the traces of its high antiquity but the following consideration is also indispensable for a proper understanding and estimate of it.

The human being of remote antiquity knows nothing about
the distinction between the mediated and immediate action of
the world creator on nature. It is thus impossible for him to
express this distinction in his language. We commonly use this
essential distinction, the fruit of a more mature reflection, since
we have described it with transcendental expressions that call
forth no pictures in one's imagination. Even if the man of the orient may have always formed this distinction in his soul, no trace
of it is visible in his language. For him, mediated and immediate
actions of God have one and the same expression. He sees God's
animating power everywhere that he turns his eyes. For him *God
plants the trees, God leads the animals* to the first human to see how
he might name them, etc. God has inspired every great truth,
every useful institution discovered by man, indeed, even every
skillful mechanical work; the *spirit of God* rests on the author or
maker. Every appearance that moves the senses has God as its
immediate cause: a *wind of God*, a *mountain of God*, a *fire of God*.
Every wise man who more or less has an inkling of the future
from the present situation of things or who definitely predicts
what will happen, every pious man who distinguishes himself
with honor is a *man of God*, a *son of God*.

The speeches of the prophets, seers, or poets—in a word, all
those who find themselves in an inspired condition—are even
bolder and more picturesque; the flourishes are generally not
only more brilliant, dazzling, and fiery, but grammar and clarity
are even sacrificed to energy and brevity, and so the meaning vac-
illates, is ambiguous and difficult to comprehend. Even more: all
animate and inanimate beings in creation intone, speak, and are
eternally in motion. Not only animals but even hills and mountains and forests *sing*. Not only do streams roar, *they clasp their
hands before God*, etc. And finally, when talk turns to the invisible,
incorporeal ruler of the world, the fiery oriental does not hesitate
to speak about him as a human being, to use expressions with
regard to him that go against our feeling and our concepts,[24] and
that have to seem all the more striking to us, since elsewhere the

24. Of the many examples that might be adduced, only one is needed to support our observation. In Psalm 78:65–6, it is said of the almighty Being: "But he
awakens from sleep like a drunken warrior and stabs his enemies in the back,"
etc. What a simile for deity!

same orators and prophets so definitely teach God's spiritual nature and warn about all idolatrous ideas. However bright and pure their concepts may be, they succumb to language, and their excited, fiery imagination leads them beyond all limits.

But to whom is it not known that the same sort of men who connect their study of languages with philosophy, good taste, and human meaning have succeeded in penetrating the spirit of the ancient authors, appreciating the quality of their symbolic expressions and, in this manner, determining their worth? Only through this means has it become possible to refute all of the distorted, hasty, and unfounded judgments that have been uttered on that score and to banish all the nonsense that a scornful wit brings to bear and all the contradictions that stupidity tries to see in this, while presenting everything in its clarity.

These advantages of exegesis and hermeneutics, of linguistic knowledge and philosophy are meanwhile lost for the teacher of religion who definitely neither wishes nor is able to regard the sacred scriptures from the relevant viewpoint. If he continues to understand the expressions of the ancient sources literally, in the sense practiced in darker centuries, while not wishing to observe the spirit of passages; if for him ancient history appears more admirable and godly the more miraculous it is and the more it contradicts the usual human conception, then he necessarily heaps up contradiction upon contradiction; the greater the struggle between truths of history and truths of reason becomes, the more he will drive the real devotees of truth away from his dogmas, since the latter individuals are convinced that one truth cannot contradict another and that the divine law book cannot require what the equally divine reason repudiates. At most, such a literalist is able to cause the true reverer of virtue to remain silent while patiently awaiting a better future, but never the latter to sacrifice his conviction—the most holy thing he possesses, like a shopkeeper's goods—to haggle shamefully over the transient goods of this world.

Does one wish to drive the thoughtful and honest inquirer into a corner, for instance, with the reproach that human reason is not able to measure up to the divine and it is one's duty to subordinate oneself blindly to the yoke of faith? This reproach cannot disturb him one moment, for the knowledge of the divinity of faith and the duty of obedience themselves belong before the

judgment seat of human reason; and if one dispossesses reason of
the judicial office we do indeed stand open to every deception
and error; thus one would sacrifice us to every trickster, to every
fanatic who has the audacity to pin his inspirations onto us as
proclamations of God.

Finally, the threat that a renounced faith will be visited with
damnation: what effect does this have on an orderly, pious mind?
For suppose we really did depend upon our reason too much,
and suppose it did really lead us away from the path of truth and
wisdom: Ought we hold such paltry concepts of the most loving
father and creator of the world that we fear he will so cruelly
punish unintentional errors? Oh, no. Let us trust him with child-
like confidence. He, who knows the thoughts of man and exam-
ines them inwardly, will pardon our false steps, bestow
forgiveness on our errors. Provided that we searched for truth,
sought the good, did the best with an honest heart and with
unfeigned conscientiousness, we can comfort ourselves with the
thought that we have fulfilled our vocation. He, who imparted to
us a limitless measure of spiritual powers; he, who implanted us
with an eternally active drive for fathoming the truth; he, who
joined the law of contradiction so firmly and inseparably to our
capacity for thought; he, who made it impossible for us to escape
this law, cannot be angry and punish if his finite creation strained
the eye of its spirit and saw nothing, inclined the ear of its mind
and heard nothing, and innocently stumbled along the path that
its creator decreed for it to wander here below. How, if the most
unjust despot doesn't demand from the lowest of his slaves some
service that exceeds the strength of his muscles, should the all-
just Being demand things from his creatures gifted with reason
that he himself has made impossible for them? To demand belief
in principles that his reason can do nothing other than repudiate?
What an idea!

We almost shrink, worthy Sir, from even mentioning in your
presence the devious path[25] of which we could avail ourselves to
reach our goal, precisely because it is a devious path and because
we consider it beneath the dignity of an honest man to proceed
other than on a straight path. One can, that is, impute another
sense to the statements that contradict the truths of reason and

25. [Eds.] *Schleifweg*.

interpret them so that every contradiction falls away. The literal words would satisfy the requirement of ecclesiastical faith, while in their meaning the principles would harmonize with the conviction of the person professing his belief. But in our situation and in our circumstances it would be deception and hypocrisy to utilize this means, even if it might be at our disposal. The result of this *Open Letter* may be whatever it will; the pious Jew and the pious Christian must always have nothing more laid at their door than an erring conscience. Wisdom and cleverness in this case uniformly demand that no appearance of double meaning, no suspicion of ambiguous action might make our undertaking impure and reprehensible. And it would be impure and reprehensible if we used the term *son of God* and other similar expressions in a dishonest manner, in a wholly different sense than Christians, in order to make them believe that we confessed their dogma.

We are by this time at the goal, worthy friend of humanity, where we must urgently request you not to withhold your counsel, your instruction, and your support from us. Duty and conscience require of us that we improve our civil condition by purifying our religious constitution but also not in any way purchase or obtain our happiness surreptitiously at the cost of truth and virtue. What we wish to do in full conviction of the rightness of our action, our descendants—and perhaps even our contemporaries—will be forced to decide to do out of necessity. For why should we, out of a misunderstood sense of delicacy, want to conceal the true condition of the great part of our brethren, especially all those who reside in the large cities? The study of Hebrew and of Talmud declines among us daily. The authority of the rabbis has diminished, and with the neglect of the ceremonial and ritual laws it must continue to diminish. In every country the government rightly has taken from these rabbis all judicial power and ecclesiastical discipline, since the civil laws of Jews no longer tolerate application in our time and the retention of excommunication and similar punishments in the hands of the scholars and theologians necessarily retards the progress of members of the community immensely.

With the bonds of religion becoming weaker, which is the lament of all religious parties, frivolousness in this regard must be expected among Jews who have no real religious instruction and no worship services that aim at piety. In addition, contacts

and social ties with Christians, which are increasingly entered
into together with the willingness of Christians to receive Jews in
their temples as fellow believers, must necessarily move the
oppressed, abandoned, and sometimes even despised Jew to convert to the Christian religion without further hesitation. In this
manner, by reciting a few words he can secure for himself all the
advantages of life, all the civil liberties that the most upright Jew
cannot attain through a lifetime of faultless behavior. This consideration is extremely disheartening for every thinking man, and
perhaps even the state authorities are not indifferent towards it.

The thinking man dares not assume that his descendants will
possess the unselfishness and strength of character to persevere
in the face of the powerful enticement of such great and so easily
attainable benefits. The authorities cannot view as desirable the
increase of such families who were either tempted out of rashness
or forced of necessity to break all family ties and who without
shame take a step that, as matters stand, has against it a universal
bias that it occurs *solely* out of self-interest.

In this labyrinth into which we have fallen through time and
circumstances, we might almost say through our very virtue, we
take refuge in you, venerable Sir. Teach us how we can find the
way out. Tell us, noble friend of virtue, if we do decide to choose
the great Protestant Christian community as a place of sanctuary:
What kind of public declaration would you, and the men who sit
with you on the venerable council, demand of us?

Or—the importance of the subject gives us the courage to
express our question even more boldly: If providence, venerable
Sir, had caused you to be born among us, and you had felt
obliged to take a similar step for similar reasons, which confession would you, with your delicate conscientiousness, have
signed or publicly declared?

Just a few words, and then we shall close.

The number of people who, full of trust, are sending this epistle
to you is quite small. Yet unless we are mistaken there must be a
sizable number of heads of families who find themselves in a similar position and who perhaps lack only an initial example to
arrive at similar decisions. This is proven by several of the
attempts, drafted by individuals of our religion, at how one might
effect a religious reform. And although we are skeptical of the
workability of these efforts, they nonetheless point unmistakably

to the need of our householders who wish to throw off the shackles of ceremonial law and, one way or the other, to incorporate themselves into the great civil society.

A definite pronouncement by a man of your stature and authority in the Christian church can thus have the most auspicious consequences for a multitude of upright, truth-loving men. By your pronouncement, noble Sir, you can promote and establish the happiness and well-being of creatures yet unborn who are capable of happiness and for whom your name will remain an eternal blessing.

The very fact that we are not taking this step merely out of consideration for ourselves helps us meet the objections that can be raised against us, objections we ourselves have raised but which we are also sure of having thoroughly laid to rest ourselves.

We can be asked, for instance, Why are you not satisfied with having disseminated morality and virtue among your people and leaving the future to Providence? The step that you are taking is astonishing. Would it not be more advisable to walk upon the slow path and to wait for time to unite all those who *serve God in spirit and in truth?* Indeed, we might be asked in addition, Do you trust so little in your wise and noble government and in the truly praiseworthy counsels of the consistory? Wouldn't they provide you with protection and assure you of tolerance once you declared your views in public? Why expose yourselves to the many judgments of those brokers of human beings that will inevitably be raised against you?

We shall answer these questions frankly. Our circle of influence is small, and however clear and pure the fundamental truths that we have made our own might be, however great and earnest our striving to establish and spread these truths among our families might be, we nevertheless cannot help but fear that the purity and innocence of these truths would not be preserved were they to be transmitted to future generations *solely by means of oral tradition.* In addition, we have never denied that our goal at the same time is to attain the rights of citizens by means of our declaration and that it is our ardent wish that in this way we may see our descendants develop their intellectual and physical powers. Therefore, if we granted that the assumption that the state will preserve and protect us is well founded, we would still always exist only as a middle thing between Jews and Christians and be

regarded and treated as a sect that, isolated and without followers, would have great difficulty existing and prospering. It would
be far too much to hope that under these circumstances we could
be accepted as citizens, attain freedom, and enter the larger society through matrimonial ties.

Finally, the history of all periods teaches that those principles
that we have called *eternal truths* are indeed the religion of individual men, but cannot long be or remain a popular religion.
These delicate flowers of the power of thought require a vessel;
and the vessel, a handle, if they are to endure and preserve their
beneficial influence. They lose their scent very easily, their blos-
soms wither, and in their decay the noblest creation of reason
becomes fatal for the spirit. Or, put in less figurative language,
when sophistry and self-interest take possession of human
beings, this system, like every other, is subject to corruption and
contamination. It therefore degenerates either into superstition
and fanaticism or into irreligion and atheism.

Without in the least seeking to anticipate your opinion, venerable Sir, we expect that the true spirit of Protestantism will shelter
and protect us and our system within its wider circle. In this way
we shall be able to attain the goal we have set for ourselves.

If the Protestant religion does indeed prescribe certain ceremonies, we can certainly resign ourselves to these as mere necessary
forms that are required for acceptance as a member into a society.
Let it be understood that we assume as a matter of principle that
these ceremonies are required merely as *actions,* as *customs,* in
order to attest: that the newly admitted member accepts the *eternal truths* out of conviction and that he submits to all the duties
that result from this as a *man* and as a *citizen.* We do not regard
this demand as a *sign* that he who performs the ceremonies is tac-
itly acknowledging that he accepts *in faith* the church *dogmas* of
this community. We would be able to comply with and fulfill that
demand with complete conscientiousness.

May, moreover, the words of the prophet *Zephaniah* thereby
come to pass: *For then I [God] will purify the language among the peoples that they may all call upon the name of the Lord, to serve Him with
one accord.*[26]

26. Zephaniah 3:9.

TWO PROTESTANT
CHRISTIAN RESPONSES
(JULY, 1799)

Friedrich Schleiermacher:
Letters on the Occasion of the Political-Theological Task and the Open Letter of Jewish Householders[1]

by a preacher outside of Berlin

Prefatory reminder of the editor

I am not able to name the author of these letters, since they are as good as being published without his knowledge, no more than I can give my own name, which would also be less than proper, since in this entire affair virtually no one has a name. They are published so late because of a rumor about a few important writings that were still to be published,[2] and I still would have happily engaged my friend in conversation about them.

These writings have appeared just now but are not of such a nature that they would have especially impressed the author, and so I offer the letters now rather than not at all. It was not necessary to print my own letters.

Berlin, July 2, 1799

---

1. *Briefe bei Gelegenheit der politisch theologischen Aufgabe und des Sendschreibens jüdischer Hausväter* (Berlin: Friedrich Franke, 1799), reprinted in Schleiermacher, *KGA* I.2: 328–61.

2. [Eds.] Probable allusion to the anonymously published works, *Beantwortung des an Herrn Probst Teller erlassenen Sendschreibens einiger Hausväter jüdischer Nation. Nicht von Teller* [Response to the Open Letter of Some Householders of the Jewish Nation to Provost Teller. Not from Teller] (Berlin 1799) and *An einige Hausväter jüdischer Religion, über die vorgeschlagene Verbindung mit den protestantischen Christen. Von einem Prediger in Berlin* [To Some Householders of the Jewish Religion, concerning the Proposed Union with Protestant Christians] (Berlin, 1799), as well as to *Lettre aux auteurs juifs d'un mémoire adressé à Mr. Teller* [Letter to Jewish Authors about a Memoir Addressed to Mr. Teller] (Berlin,1799) by Jean André de Luc, all of which appeared before Teller's answer.

First Letter

P. . . , April 17, 1799

Thank you, indeed, dear friend, for sending me the *Open Letter* so soon. I had just read the *Political-Theological Task*, which I had mislaid, and was still caught up with many ideas about it when your letter arrived with the *Open Letter*. So now my thinking about the whole affair can proceed in one piece, and, as you can easily imagine, I shall be heartily pleased to get rid of it all the sooner. For me there is nothing like engaging in my speculations, about which you so happily amuse yourself from the height of your lofty life of business affairs. If I get involved in these speculations, of course I know that I have only myself to depend upon, and yet I'll find my way out of it in the end. But these matters from practical life are quite well suited to torment an honest man. Not you, of course, but the rest of us, who can do nothing but think and speak about them, which means achieving nothing nowadays. On all sides one bumps into sharp corners and rubs oneself raw on the rough spots of the age—with the splendid advantage that one does not cast about in empty space but is offset by something. That means if one believes he has an idea on the matter and wishes to express it, then you politicians come along and, with a secretive and superior air, admonish us that we are not allowed to understand the whole affair, which nonetheless is usually of the sort that one rightly can demand that every reasonable person should understand it. After all, you have yourself often treated me so; and such treatment has, of course, long been the great battle-cry of our statesmen.

Meanwhile, I should have thought that it is not a matter of high-flown presumptions for us to want to know why, and owing to which of our characteristics, we actually can be what we, by the grace of God and the state, truly are in this most real of worlds. You see, as much as I delight in being a citizen with one's due rights, and neither more nor less, it still disturbs me greatly and often interrupts my enjoyment that I really do not know why I of all people should have and be so much. And that knowledge really should not be granted to me, for if I only knew why it can be granted to me, then I would also have to understand the reasons why it can't be granted to the Jews, and we poor laypersons in the art of statecraft certainly are not supposed to want to judge.

Do not reprimand me about my indolence and indifference toward all these things; I only wish I were at that stage again, and then at least this affair would be off my mind. But our neighbors left and right see to it sufficiently that one cannot get any real rest. Meanwhile, I cannot say that the *Open Letter* would have brought me appreciably closer to this end as regards my aim and goal: it has neither opened up more pleasant prospects for my good will nor quickened my thoughts in a new direction, whether forwards, or in a circle—in brief, I must confess to you that I cannot share your sense of the matter's great importance. This time we diverge quite far from one another, but that may well be because we haven't spoken about such things for a long time and also because you judge things precisely from the standpoint of the state, or at least your official residence, while I, who know next to nothing anymore about the latter and what occurs there, can only form an opinion according to the general view of things.

Who can deny that the *Open Letter* is, at any rate, beautifully written? And you know what great delight I can take in everything that does honor to the older school of our literature. The starting point that it takes about mysticism—even if it be the case that its author starts back too far—is very agreeable to me:[3] I still own up to my old love, and a well-crafted panegyric on that always seems to me to be appropriate. I also cannot concede to you that this passage merely hovers over the whole, like a calligraphic squiggle; it clearly belongs to the historical, which is the pedestal of the entire writing. Yes, exactly, a pedestal—for it isn't connected more precisely with the main building. And this main building?—Well then, if you were to ask me about it, it seems like a pyramid that by nature becomes ever narrower, and so it is no misfortune that the pinnacle is broken off.[4] I also happily admit to you that it will create more of a sensation than the former essay,[5] which was only hastily thrown out to the public. Yet if this is

3. [Eds.] Cross-references to the preceding translations are cited respectively as *T* for "Task" and as *OL* for *Open Letter*; *OL*, 42–4; *Sendschreiben* 3–7, *KGA* I.2: 382, 3–383, 38. Schleiermacher recognizes that Friedländer's letter is grounded both in his personal history and in an historical account of his tradition.

4. [Eds.] Friedländer's argument is richer and more extensive in treating Judaism than in making his actual proposal to convert to Protestant Christianity.

5. [Eds.] The "Political-Theological Task."

directed to a famous theologian,[6] he must, in the end, answer. That may provide a means of dramatic involvement and arouse interest; but if I may say so, I doubt this whole thing may actually be more and that something more at all than this sensation may be intended by it. In fact, I have not been able to understand what you mean by saying that this is not merely something *spoken,* as is the *Task;* but that something is really supposed to *happen.* What is supposed to happen? Do you consider an exchange of writings with Mr. Teller a fact in any other than the literary sense?[7] After all, he and the other men of the "venerable council"[8] are not one and the same; and even if they were, their answer obtained in this manner would only be a private opinion, and the *Open Letter* writer and his friends would not come one step further in what they wanted to do—even if they wanted something else. Mr. Teller and our entire Supreme Consistory can found no new sect on their own authority and cannot even alter the age-old customs of the hitherto acknowledged ecclesiastical societies.

A document that at the same time seeks to be a step forward must wherever possible come from an authority—just remember how bad it was that during the last reform plan the representatives of Judaism, in the end, had to admit they had no competent authority—but certainly go to an authority, I mean a civil authority, and, as we know, the higher, the more desirable. Thus an open letter to the king from a number of important men would clearly be a deed! And the fine features of this would not need to be lost to the world; it would surely not be the first petition to him that would merely be secretly handed over afterwards to the press. Or do you understand by "deed" the actual proposal of the householders, the quasi-conversion? I would like to call it the plot of the drama. If it is therewith really true, then I now find nothing so very important in it other than that some reasonable and educated Jews want to use Christianity as a means of entering civil society. After all, the procedure is otherwise the usual one, only

6. [Eds.] Wilhelm Abraham Teller.

7. [Eds.] See *Gedanken* 1, Nr. 205; *KGA* I.2: 47, 1–3: "They [the Jews] think Teller should answer in the name of the consistory since they could really not even answer as delegated [*Deputirte*] in the name of their fellow believers [*Committenten*]."

8. [Eds.] See *OL,* 76; *Sendschreiben* 81, *KGA* I.2: 411, 4.

that in their honesty they distinguish themselves by a more sub-tle eudaemonism—for alongside their self-preservation they also speak about the preservation of posterity—and that they inquire about the most civil and intellectual price of the good they seek newly to acquire. All this I would have thought they might have been able to arrange quietly.

But if the householders are a fiction, this form conceals from the public the correct standpoint for judging the document. Since only an isolated case is set forth favorably, one notices less how for this writer the basis of it all is actually the sad and despairing belief that no other means to gain equality with other citizens remains open to the Jews than conversion to Christianity, which one should seek to arrange as easily as possible. Those good men[9]—who in former times worked zealously in another way for the civil improvement of their nation—how insulted they must feel that one man, who is truly beyond dispute one of the most prominent of their well-informed brethren, maintains publicly in such a significant manner that at that time they had been on a completely false path and that the nation would have to give up all hope of getting further on this path! How deeply wounded must especially the splendid Friedländer[10] feel! I am curious whether he will not stand up and raise his voice against this betrayal of the better cause; he, who at that time departed from the battleground with such great hopes,[11] as it seemed at least, who—a more authentic follower of Mendelssohn than this man here—didn't even want to hear anything about the abolition of the ceremonial law but insisted decisively that not even Jewish orthodoxy could hinder the enfranchisement of his people. Yet in this matter allow yourself to give the author of the *Open Letter* cre-dence over Friedländer, as I believe that the former proposition

9. [Eds.] See *OL*, 76; *Sendschreiben* 82, *KGA* I.2: 411, 17–22, where Friedländer alludes to his own earlier reform efforts of 1792–3.

10. [Eds.] It is a moot question whether Schleiermacher knew that Friedländer was the author of the *Open Letter* at the time he wrote his response; to have cited Friedländer against the document was, in any case, a clever rhetorical ploy, since Schleiermacher was well aware of how the *Open Letter* deviates from Friedländer's expressed antipathy to conversion to Christianity. On the ambiguity of Friedländer's character see Lowenstein, *Crisis of Berlin Jewry.*

11. [Eds.] Friedländer's compilation of his efforts is found in *Akten-Stücke die Reform der Jüdischen Kolonien in den Preußischen Staaten betreffend* (Berlin, 1793).

might not be defensible in its entire strictness. Why then should there be a great leap into Christianity over all the possibilities that lie in between? And why, to be sure, as ungraciously as it occurs here, together with the most serious protestations against Christianity and under the strangest gestures that clearly show that neither love for the new nor hate toward the old religion is the cause of this cumbersome change but only the push of external authority or, rather, fear of it, and belief in it?

Reason demands that all should be citizens, but it does not require that all must be Christians, and thus it must be possible in many ways to be a citizen and a non-Christian—which surely any number of them already have become—and to discover among them that way that is suited to our situation and the case at hand; that is the task that no one can escape who wishes to speak openly about this matter and that thus far has not been treated such that one might let it rest as settled. If it is a lazy use of reason (*ratio ignava Kantii*)[12] to hold that something desirable is impossible because it hasn't yet succeeded, how should it not be a case of irresponsible cowardice to give up on that very thing that is known to be not only desirable but necessary? Why give it up now, not only since it has already begun in other lands but also since our own state has made a praiseworthy attempt therewith, merely because the conditions under which it occurred in these first efforts are for us partly not desirable and partly not possible?

Whoever does not wish to contribute to the final and satisfactory solution of this task directly by making new proposals or by seeking to resolve difficulties that one could not overcome until now, must—if one doesn't just tell him that he ought to remain silent—at least make an indirect contribution. He must tackle things in their present situation, bring forth the incoherence and inconsistencies in the present conduct of so-called Christian states, and place things in some kind of new light; he must apply some kind of stimulus to tease them out of their laziness so that

12. [Eds.] On Kant's notion of lazy reason, see the *Critique of Pure Reason*, tr. Norman Kemp Smith (London: Macmillan, 1961), 561–2 [B 717]: "We may so entitle every principle which makes us regard our investigation into nature, on any subject, as absolutely complete, disposing reason to cease from further enquiry, as if it had entirely succeeded in the task which it had set itself."

they finally begin to make proposals from their side and—which
they alone are capable of—proceed at the same time with the
work at hand. In our case, the government, whose passivity is
otherwise not to be lamented, has consistently remained inactive.
With the exception of the New East-Prussian Regulation of the
Jews,[13] all essential proposals and initiatives have come forth
either from the Jews themselves or otherwise from private persons, from theorizing minds or practical friends of humanity. You
know that I do not share the sorry judgment that the state only
pursues the affair in this negligent manner in order not to lose
protection money,[14] and that to me this view is in complete conflict with the character of our government; but it is all the same a
lazy use of reason by men of affairs, which views the remains of
ancient barbarism as indestructible and the collisions that can
arise from this affair, which are really considerable enough, as
irresolvable. But things cannot remain this way, and the state
must at some point begin to press on with the matter as a freely
pursued activity. If one finds it astounding to go out on con-
quests—which of course always have political reasons—as long
as there are still wastelands to make arable and marshes to dry
out within one's own borders, how should one not find it infinitely strange to bring in foreigners from outside as citizens, as
long as there are still a large number of persons within who are

13. [Eds.] The *General-Juden-Reglement für Süd- und Neu-Ost-Preußen* from April
17, 1797, is printed in Rönne/Simon: *Die Verfassung und Verwaltung des Preußischen Staates*, Bd 8/3. *Die früheren und gegenwärtigen Verhältnisse der Juden in den
sämmtlichen Landestheilen des Preußischen Staates* (Breslau, 1843), 292–302. This document treats the toleration and protection of Jews living in the Prussian regions of
South- and New-East Prussia. Its provisions regulate travel, business, rights and
types of residency, occupations, taxes (which are put on a parity with those of
gentiles in the region of equivalent social standing), and the practices of religion
and worship, where Jews are protected "in the free practice of their religion and
shall not be disturbed either in their public or their domestic customs of worship"
(299). The regulation was superceded by French law in the Treaty of Tilsit, July 12,
1807, when these regions were lost as a result of the Napoleonic wars.

14. [Eds.] *Schutzgeld*. Werner E. Mosse writes that legally protected Jews had to
pay a "price for every privilege granted to them." See "From '*Schutzjuden*' to
'*Deutsche Staatsbürger Jüdischen Glaubens*': The Long and Bumpy Road of Jewish
Emancipation in Germany," in *Paths of Emancipation: Jews, States, and Citizenship*,
ed. Pierre Birnbaum and Ira Katznelson (Princeton: Princeton University Press,
1995), 61.

actually not yet citizens?[15] Behind what is this lazy reasoning hiding, other than behind the dogma about the inner corruption of the Jews and behind the maxim that it is therefore dangerous to accept them into civil society? I have found this belief still very widespread among men of your estate. God knows how this belief may have been shaped into a full-blown theory in the matters they have thought and written about in their official duties, about which little is ever reported to the public; a belief that goes around in a strange circle with the maxim built upon it and would certainly yield other and progressive results, if one were as far along in an enlightened policy as we are in contemptible theology so that, for example, one might nicely illuminate dogmas historically.

When I saw the historical aspects of the *Open Letter*, I entertained some hope in that direction, but in vain. You know how much has been said back and forth on this topic without it ever having borne any fruit; and now you wonder whether anything else remains for a poor author than to proceed from this very hypothesis, to show that the present manner of acting runs counter to it and that the gallantry that the state exercises in relation to the Christian church, by connecting the enjoyment of all civil rights to the conversion to it, truly contradicts that dogma. The feeling of self-contradiction is usually a powerful inducement for healthy beings, and one must attempt to stimulate it, if this can happen merely by means of the cutting edge of dialectic and biting, caustic satire. From this standpoint I have examined the *Political-Theological Task* and believe that more appropriate things are thereby intended—and, if one only speaks loudly and distinctly enough, might also be achieved—than through the idealized picture of a pure Judaism and the appended and rather inappropriately put question of a pure or, more likely, an empty Christianity.

I only wish that the author might not have depended so much on the respondents to his question[16] but might have also at least

15. [Eds.] A possible allusion to the 1797 law regulating Jewish life in the territories acquired by Prussia as a result of the Prussian and Russian partitioning of Poland in 1792, 1793, and 1795.

16. [Eds.] The last section of Schleiermacher's *First Letter* combines references to Friedländer's letter with arguments from "Political-Theological Task." See *OL*, 76; *Sendschreiben* 81, *KGA* I.2: 411,3–11: "What kind of public declaration would you, and the men who sit with you on the venerable council, demand of us?"

touched on the objections one could make to his main propositions.[17] It's perfectly obvious that the state, according to its own
theory, mustn't view the proselytes whom the Christian church
makes from Judaism in the present situation as a peculiar acquisition, if it is going to judge morally—which is then also presup-
posed. But hasn't it already been the last refuge of our
Enlighteners, when they become aware now and again that their
business just won't get on, to give up the present generation and
to dedicate their efforts exclusively to future generations? When
none of the popular writings and popular speeches help at all,
then the unfortunate philanthropist throws himself into peda-
gogy and catechesis. Shall one not ascribe these maxims to the
state for its defense? Will one not have to let it answer: "The state
knows quite well that the Israelites who convert to Christianity
do not give up their innate corruption; it would ascribe such
power neither to the water of holy baptism nor to the other moral
aids of Christians in which they might be able to take part; but it
would at least wish to maintain oversight over the evil that they
bring with them in order at least to save their progeny. These
would no longer be able to grow up in the principles of Jewish
immorality. Like other children, they would drink in a pure
morality and a great reverence for the fatherland in our excellent
schools, where affairs of the fatherland dominate everywhere as
substance, and everything is poured into moral form." This
Enlightenment mannerism has always seemed contemptible to
me, since I believe less in the effectiveness of persuasion than in
shrewdness, in having a good eye, and in the powers of observation of children. But if in certain things this mannerism appears
to succeed—as in cases where our schools in their recently begun
eternal war against parental example and domestic education
have already produced some trophies—then it is to be credited
least in what the state views as the moral and political corruption
of the Jews. This actually should have been questioned and
shown more sharply in the *Task*, i.e., that so long as the state

17. [Eds.] Schleiermacher is wary of the proposal in the *Task* for a time of edu-
cating Jewish converts' moral character [*Bildungszeit*], since the satire appears to
lapse rhetorically into accepting the assumption of Jewish moral depravity. His
second letter strongly defends the author's outrage over the age-old European
belief in Jewish moral corruption and seeks to ward off misinterpretations of the
document's intent.

views Judaism and anticivil sentiment as equivalents—for that is still its only real concern in the matter—it mustn't also adopt this maxim. I want to avoid speaking further with you about matters in which my thoughts have long been known to you, and I shall now stop altogether in order not to fall into one of my old, familiar laments, about which I may already have carried on enough to make you alarmed. Farewell!

Second Letter

P. . . , the 24th of April, 1799

So the sharp tone of the *Task* and the rage that is visible in it displease you, and for this reason you commend to me the dignified seriousness with which the *Open Letter* is composed? Are you serious, or is that your dignified joke? And do you only wish to represent a general opinion, perhaps in your locale, in opposition to mine? So little does it sound like you that I am necessarily left to conjecture, especially about all the things that, to my great astonishment, you tell me in your letter. So it is not a mere rhetorical fiction or a prophecy, but a fact, that one trades religion on the open market.[18] It looks like it is about to be practiced on an even larger scale, since there are Jews who wish to have their children circumcised and at the same time baptized. There are now already amphibians whose nature might be difficult to determine. It is true that the greatest foolishness reveals itself in almost every example of a change of religion. You know all that and yet require that a political inconsistency that has such important and sad results arouse no indignation, and also that one is not supposed to give voice to the matter in the strongest and most pronounced terms.

18. [Eds.] See *T*, 37; *Politisch-theologische Aufgabe, KGA* I.2: 377,41–378,6: "As soon as he makes a claim to monetary reward, to liberation from accustomed limitations, to acquisition of new rights, the purity, together with the greatness of his action, is cast aside. He sinks down to the depraved class of people who sacrifice themselves and their worth for small restitution and barter away the feeling for eternal truths for lower sensual enjoyment. No one guarantees that under changed situations and circumstances, if he does not find the rate of exchange of the religious belief he just left more advantageous, he would not once again exchange this religious belief without any scruples, under many sorts of pretexts."

After reading your letter I confess that I still would all too happily have brought some good and proper emphasis into the
harangue against proselytes. You are correct that too strong and
unconditional an accent is placed on the disruption of families;[19]
but being correct can still be only of limited use. When an important and moral topic is at stake it would be silly if a reasonable
person were only to pay attention to the limited way of thinking
of those who hold that all contact and all love, possibly referring
to some other points of union, would have to cease if someone
steps out of the one point. But why should a serious, liberal man
still consider the petty, for the most part, mercantilistic self-interest and the usually just as petty inclinations to be important topics? Why should everyone treat social sentiments like an
exchange of coins, where one is indifferent about where they
come from as long as he only receives them?

Yet you don't like the whole style, and in this you are wrong. If
only it were more strongly delineated; for I am concerned that
many persons will think the author has adopted the political
hypothesis in earnest and is a real enemy of the Jews. Look how
the dry and cold argumentation in no way mitigates the inconsistency. One would then have to be so good natured as to think it
does not know it is inconsistent, which certainly very seldom
takes place. Otherwise the inconsistency is still actually a victory—and, to be sure, a conscious victory—of different motives
over the power of the context. One thus has to set up other
motives for this; one has to make the contradiction felt, and I do
not see how that can otherwise be done.

Yet I nonetheless want to have justified not only the *Task* but
also the *Open Letter* itself, insofar, of course, as its dignified ear-
nestness is not quite as you imagine. But what colors the earnest-
ness does not please me nearly as much as the honest satire of
the *Task*, because in the *Open Letter* it is a more restrained, and
actually just as deep but more timid, bitterness that does not
dare to step forth so boldly. Everything that has to do with Judaism is, of course, treated with much dignity and seriousness. In
the section on mysticism Judaism is treated out of pure opposition to the theological-pedagogical Enlightenment. This is an

19. [Eds.] See *T* 36–7; *Politisch-theologische Aufgabe, KGA* I.2: 377,1–23, for a most
poignant expression of the personal and social costs of conversion to Christianity.

opposition that the greatest part of the educated world certainly only pardons in a Jew, so I would advise a Christian who wishes to say such a thing to pretend to be a Jew. In the historical section, Judaism is treated with pure respect, all the more so because many details by their nature border on the amusing. Thus one readily arrives at the view that the "authentic meaning"[20] attributed to all ceremonies may in most cases have been "authentic" only for the priests; one is only prevented from this and similar considerations by its thoroughly uniform, serious tone. But wherever the state and Christianity are touched upon, I find that restrained bitterness; and the appearance of quiet dignity, which you, along with many others, find in this part of the work, seems to me not at all to proceed from the spirit of the writing or its author, but I view it as a well-intended yet hard-to-explain product of the reader himself. It is in fact a remarkable good fortune that not every document encounters, least of all an anonymous one, where no favorable prejudices can come to one's aid, that the *Open Letter* is, as you say, so widely praised; and due to the beautiful style both parties seem either not to notice or wholly to forget many things that should surely give offense to both. Yet I for one have not found the work so deceptive or so charming. If you earnestly do not wish to believe in this bitterness, consider nonetheless that the author, however willing he may be to throw off the ceremonial law,[21] still only raises the demand to convert to Christianity as an obtrusive, unwarranted expectation of the Christians, and it is perfectly clear to you that a man of such honesty, by yielding to it, cannot remain in a peaceful state of mind.

Recall how the greatest loyalty to the original Abrahamic Judaism, for a Judaism yet to be renewed but still not at hand, shines through; and how this Judaism, as is fair, is placed completely in opposition to Christianity; how the author imports the basic truths of his religion from Judaism[22] and thus likewise his doubts

20. [Eds.] *OL*, 53; *Sendschreiben* 30; *KGA* I.2: 392,3

21. [Eds.] See *OL*, 67; *Sendschreiben* 60; *KGA* I.2: 403,11–15: "Taken together, all these reasons insist, with united strength, on casting off the burdensome yoke of ceremonial and ritual laws, whose abolition the lawgiver himself would teach and enjoin if he lived in our times."

22. [Eds.] See *OL*, 50–1; *Sendschreiben* 22–4; *KGA* I.2: 389,6–35

about Christianity;[23] how he reproaches the ceremonial law, not
because he moves beyond the authorities of Judaism but because
this repudiation agrees with Moses and all the rabbis;[24] how he
pardons Judaism for its lack from religious instruction, because
this concurs with the freedom from symbols[25] and presses Christianity about the moral dangers of dogmas, which then go
unmentioned out of forbearance;[26] how he nevertheless wishes to
derive a morality contrary to ours from the prophets and psalms,
as a proper extract, however much this great historical imputa-
tion fights against it;[27] how the Christians cling to their basic
truths only as belief, while theirs are presented as inner convictions, and the most violent exegesis of the sort only our wildest
neologists ever allowed themselves is here applied throughout in
order to defend Judaism.

Recall all that, and you will be just as little inclined as I to
doubt the author's honest hatred of Christianity. In the individual
expressions that sound so peaceful—for example, about the "ever
open portals of the Christian temple; about the similarly open
arms and the ever ready philanthropic hearts of members of the
large religious society; about the wide range of Protestantism or
about Christian teachers, who would gladly and without second
thought accept the confession of the householders, if not as identical, yet as in agreement with the faith of the church"[28]—and in
whatever other similar material presents itself, you will also just
find precisely this restrained bitterness. All of this taken together
brings me to the thought that the author cannot be serious even
by half in the way he proposes conversion to Christianity; rather
that his intention is only to proceed in such a way as to make it
obvious that such a half-way transition is the most that could be
demanded of a reasonable and educated man, quite apart from
the fact that one should not require anything of the kind. This

23. [Eds.] See *OL*,73–5; *Sendschreiben* 73–8; *KGA* I.2: 408,8–409,40

24. [Eds.] See *OL*, 53–4, 57, 67; *Sendschreiben* 28–9, 31, 36, 60; *KGA* I.2: 391,20–31; 392,23–32; 394,20–4; 403,11–5.

25. [Eds.] Friedländer, *Akten-Stücke* 21

26. [Eds.] See *OL*, 62; *Sendschreiben* 47–8; *KGA* I.2: 398,21–32.

27. [Eds.] See *OL*, 63; *Sendschreiben* 50; *KGA* I.2: 399,16–23

28. [Eds.] Partly paraphrased from *OL*, 69;*Sendschreiben* 64–5; *KGA* I.2: 404, 27–39.

secret meaning will satisfy the Jewish nation, which is so clever in matters of interpretation, whereas the letter and the appearance of peace and dignity is for the Christians; the former to embarrass them, the latter to keep them in a good mood. And this thought would be good enough and the best that could happen from the standpoint of the author and, in addition, the most natural, except that too great an ignorance of Christianity has hindered the real execution of the matter. As far as its doubts about our religion go, this passage strikingly resembles the whole work, so that after impressive preparations it amounts to something very small. I am pleased to confess to you that I could not refrain from laughing when, after this great debate about the genius of the original language and the principles of Mendelssohn's philosophy, I found the author suddenly at his goal[29] with the doctrine of the Son of God and with his solemn protestation against it.

So that is the great reservation? And nothing more? My God, does the man know nothing about the ancient and modern history of Christianity and the weight which one has conferred—not only with eyes half closed but also in the most formal manner— on this dogma, and the opinions held about it for quite some time? Yet tell me, do all enlightened and learned Jews—who actually expect us to know something about Judaism and to find something tasteful in Chaldean wisdom and beauty, no matter how contrary it is to our European spirit, as I have often found in printed essays—do they all know so incredibly little about Christianity? Then on this they appear to me somewhat—to be sure, in a much grander fashion—like the French, who now have already lived among us for ten years and are still unable to learn a proper word of German.[30] That, I might let pass; what does it concern me? But anyone who writes to Mr. Teller—especially insofar as he is a prominent teacher of religion—for that writer, it is quite unpardonable not to know why Teller, among other things, is just that. Or if he knows, it is even more unpardonable when he tells him "that there are principles in Protestant Christianity that contradict the truths of reason and that one can overcome this

29. [Eds.] See *OL*, 75; *Sendschreiben* 78; *KGA* I.2: 409,40

30. [Eds.] See *Gedanken* 1, Nr. 209; *KGA* I.2: 47,13–4: "Jews who do not concern themselves with Christianity are like the French who don't want to learn German."

contradiction only through a devious path, which is beneath the dignity of an honest man"[31] and that if one took the term "Son of God" and other similar expressions in the sense of the original language, one would use them in a quite different sense from the Christians, which would be a great hypocrisy. So it goes at times, when similarly "the law of contradiction is still joined so firmly and inseparably to our capacity of thinking."[32] Here the author of the *Open Letter* has let himself get carried away much too far, even beyond the bounds of good manners. And it has to be Mr. Teller, of all people, upon whose tone in responding these statements (which I would truly be at a loss to characterize) are supposed to have no influence whatsoever. Be sure to send it to me as soon as it appears.

Third Letter

P. . . , the 2nd of May, 1799

In view of my claims to inaction and distance from all worldly affairs and with the firm conviction I have that nothing beneficial will come from this whole movement, it is for me quite amazing how much lively participation I have bestowed on the entire matter. But you err in your supposition; I believe I myself have come closer to the truth of the matter. You know that hope does not move me or drive me out of my sphere as much as fear, and so also I have fared on this occasion. You proceed from the position that I could generally make no objection to the conversions of Jews if it were only to happen in an appropriate manner, and I am myself aware that this very thing is the subject of my concern. I fear that if the *Open Letter*, as I would assume to be necessarily and generally known, has no effect on the situation of the Jews in the common realm, and this common realm takes either no notice or not the desired notice of the proposal made, then the practices taken hitherto will catch on further. Individual persons and whole families

---

31. [Eds.] Reformulated from *OL*, 74–5; *Sendschreiben* 77; *KGA* I.2: 409,20–6. Schleiermacher's formulation reads the *Open Letter* in a manner that conceals the fact that Friedländer actually rejects the (devious) path that would verbally confess Christ as Son of God while putting an interpretation on these words that robs the expression of its uniqueness.

32. [Eds.] See *OL*, 74; *Sendschreiben* 76; *KGA* I.2: 409,8–9.

will more frequently convert to Christianity in the usual manner, and this is what I quite seriously take to be the worst thing that can happen. If you put yourself in my position as a Christian and listen to my reasons, you will surely see that I am right.

Twenty or thirty years ago there was nothing to say about this statute of Christian states, by virtue of which a Jew, as soon as he becomes a Christian, is also a citizen; and I would have lost no words over the use that was made of it at that time. Both religious parties were so separated from one another, and the Jews so very stripped of everything that could have made them capable of some other manner of life, that the temptation to merge with the Christians and to disperse themselves among the various branches of civic activities could not possibly be widespread among many, or even a matter of strong urgency for more than a few. Of course, there were now and then some proselytes but— apart from the infatuated, if I may exempt them—there were really bad characters of whom the Jewish community was all too glad to rid itself; persons who were ruined and brought to despair or such persons who only had a momentary advantage in view, and yet, thanks be to God, there are always only a few of these. Most were immediately reduced to poor-relief or to the private charity of their new partners in faith, in that they went begging with their baptismal certificate, which had been their actual venture, like a letter of permission to seek alms after a fire.[33] Others had taken aim at the curiosity of well-intended souls, who, for the sake of divine things, were pleased to get a bargain on learning some bad Hebrew. Of course, it was a misfortune when such a man turned up, and I have often heard your uncle and my father complain that in the name of the church they could never completely renounce a person who manifested a desire for instruction, no matter how bad he might be. For all that, these people, whatever their standing with their faith might be, were too insignificant to do damage to the church. Even if through their conduct they caused scandal enough for the church because of their thoroughly bad character, the reproach that the church had attracted them out of its zeal for proselytes was quite unthinkable.

---

33. [Eds.] *Brandbrief*, an official letter that authorizes victims of a fire to solicit funds. *Duden Deutsches Universal Wörterbuch* (Mannheim: Dudenverlag, 1983), 217.

Now that is all completely different and actually so much the worse, the more dazzling it all is. Quite different people now proceed to convert to Christianity; educated and well-to-do persons, well versed in worldly matters, wish to acquire rights and become citizens. For them, the very thing that is pointed out to them from afar as the reward of their conversion is an important and long sought-after object. It may be that their conversion does not harm the state so much, which, as far as I am concerned, is responsible for itself and can do as it pleases. Nonetheless, as is shown by the *Task*'s own supposition, it harms the church and Christianity all the more. By far most of those whom we can expect among us will be the sort of persons who are wholly indifferent towards anything having to do with religion, either because they are against its moral customs and completely ruled by worldly convictions or because, saturated in Kantian wisdom, they are only concerned with their own morality. As far as Christianity goes, having only their political purpose in view, they listen to everything said to them about it with only half an ear or not at all, and after their instruction and their baptism they know just as little and are just as far from it as before. If only I could for a moment make you not into a cleric but simply into a Christian, so that you might respond to my question from this perspective: What are we to do with such people? In dealing with a precious and volatile substance one does not usually try to preserve a small quantity in an extremely large vessel, for it will completely lose its strength there and dissipate into the surrounding air. Likewise, it is highly dangerous when only a small quantity of religion comes to rest or circulate in an extremely large religious society, not only because then—however little anyone would actually do this—so much external religion is set in motion behind which there is nothing. It thereby happens that those who are or should remain outside believe that this is religion, as they otherwise see nothing. However, it is also dangerous because the advantages of the religious society for the few who are in possession of religion get completely lost by being scattered around this great, as it were, empty space: they do not perceive and can have no affect on one another.

Unfortunately, even among old Christians there are too many who do not set good examples for newer Christians but only belong to some sort of church for the sake of the necessary baptismal certificate, of opportunities and the like, or for the sake of the

Westphalian Peace,[34] and who for the most part are wholly inno-
cent of any inclination towards religion. I wished there were
some good way that we might get rid of all of them, and for a
long while I have looked around for acceptable proposals to
accomplish this. But if their numbers should be increased signifi-
cantly by people of whom many have no small influence in the
society, I would consider this highly dangerous; I am even
inwardly convinced that it would bring the religious society
close to ruin. For not only would most of our newer members be
irreligious, but all, in some fashion, would also be anti-Christian.
I can imagine the "awakened youths"[35]—of whom, as the author
says, in all fairness there are supposed to be very many (though
surely there are only very few)—in no other way than as coming
from his school. For he would probably not allow the Kantian-
affected to count, since he scornfully took no notice of this philosophy in the presentation of his basic truths (although I have been
assured that one could scarcely find three or four younger, educated Jewish householders, among whom in every case there is
not at least one Kantian). If Judaism and its spirit are now so
deeply seated in their leader, a philosophically thinking man,
that he would always remain a Jew even if he somehow under-
went baptism, what is to be expected from the others, from
whom one cannot to the same degree anticipate that they, likewise through self-formation,[36] will have destroyed the work of
their instruction? They would therefore not bring to us a capacity
for Christianity and therefore would acquire none among us. In
this regard there can be no talk about some trial years,[37] even if
there were twenty. It is impossible for anyone who really has a
religion to accept another one; and if all Jews were most excellent

34. [Eds.] The Peace of Westphalia (1648), which brought the Thirty Years' War
to an end, re-affirmed the territorial religious settlement of the Peace of Augsburg
(1555) but also provided a general amnesty for all who had been deprived of their
rights because of religious affiliations or political activities.

35. [Eds.] See OL, 46; Sendschreiben 11; KGA I.2: 385,14–5.

36. [Eds.] Selbstbildung; see Schleiermacher, On Religion, Speech 3, "On Self-Formation for Religion," 55–71.

37. [Eds.] See T, 38–9, where the author proposes a six-year period for the
moral cultivation of new Jewish converts; Politisch-theologische Aufgabe 237; KGA
I.2: 378,35. In this passage Schleiermacher again plays the arguments of the one
document off against the other.

citizens, not a single one of them would be a good Christian, but
they would bring along a great many peculiarly Jewish elements
in their religious principles and convictions that, just for this reason, are anti-Christian.[38]

Indeed, a judaizing Christianity would be the true disease
with which we should infect ourselves![39] You are not such a lay-
man in church history that you are not able to remember how in
ancient and modern times of Christianity all sorts of harm arose
wholly from this source, which always continues to trickle
steadily when one thought it had long since been cut off, harm
from which we have freed ourselves with the greatest effort and
in a forceful manner, and from which we are still not wholly free.
Moreover, those who are not even Jews would, nevertheless, for
the most part probably bring along a multitude of Jewish prejudices and superstitions, if it is otherwise permitted to judge them
by Christians who are actually not even Christians. With such
persons—and not only with the common run—a good dose of
superstition and prejudices stemming from the religiosity of
former times survive, and why should this be any less the case
with the Jews? We would thus also have to grapple with them!

You see, that would be the damage, a damage not to be overcome, that Christianity would have if the Jews, in whatever manner, were to unite with it merely for the reason that the
government is so courteous as to make it a condition for civil liberty! It is already a highly tedious duty in our social life that now
and then one finds it necessary to accept something unpleasant in
an agreeable manner and with the appearance of satisfaction and
gratefulness simply because someone believes he is doing us a

38. [Eds.] *Gedanken* 1, Nr. 204; *KGA* I.2: 46,18–9: "In the *Open Letter* the tendency is present to be a people of God, first while continuing to deduce their natural religion from Moses, and second while they want to overcome the burden of
believing in Christ. They can have intended nothing other than beneath it all to
want to say: even the enlightened Christian still remains a Christian. But one can
also at the same time say about them: even the most enlightened Jew still remains
a Jew."

39. [Eds.] Schleiermacher's sarcasm follows Paul's stance in Galatians 2–3,
which polemicizes against a judaizing, i.e., legalistic, Christianity. Even as a
mature theologian, Schleiermacher expresses an aversion to the Hebraic scriptures that plays a significant role in his theology; what strikes one here is that he
grasps the social-political situation of his Jewish contemporaries with such empathy despite this aversion.

favor with it; and what one usually takes away from that experience is that one must subsequently endure it from time to time so
as not to contradict oneself. But in important relationships this is
really a highly dangerous and unreasonable maxim. I am, as you
know, generally quite cynical on such occasions; I thank someone
in a friendly manner for his good will and, without much ado, say
that nothing in the matter concerns me. It seems to be high time
for the Christian church to act similarly; for if it endures this all-
the-more decadent governmental courtesy even longer, it will
pay, much too dearly indeed, for this politeness with its complete
ruin. In addition, consider now that beyond such damage the
church will also have substantial scandal from it, which it can
similarly ill afford. After all, it's to no purpose to want to deny
that Jews increasingly take part in education in our times in
roughly the same way as Christians do, that they depart more and
more from foreign elements in their customs and conduct, and,
what is best, that their very honesty grows more prominent,
which is the natural consequence of a secure well-being, when
better sociability and a feeling of honor are able to work on the
mind. The more all this is the case, the more that very thing disappears that could serve to illustrate the alleged lawfulness of a civil
distinction between Jews and Christians and the more the contin-
uation of this distinction resembles groundless partisanship.

If one now sees in other states, and especially in those that
have ceased to be Christian, how emancipation has proceeded
swiftly and without difficulties,[40] then necessarily among those
who lack sufficient religious sense to grasp the damage that the
church really suffers, the common judgment must in the end prevail that only the personal Christian nature of regents and servants of the state or the secretive law-making power of public
opinion built on religious principles might stand opposed to this
important state business. So now the church can be accused of
making proselytes, and it must hasten to free itself from this suspicion through some powerful step. Whatever Teller as a private
citizen may respond to these private citizens in his doctrinal wisdom, it appears to me now to be high time that the Christian
church, officially through its overseers and spokespersons

40. [Eds.] An allusion to revolutionary France's antipathy to religion and its
emancipation of French Jews.

appointed by the state and individually through its most prominent teachers, publicly and wherever possible should decisively
declare itself to this effect: that it request the state to put an end to
such an oppressive course of action; that it implore the state by its
love of Christianity—of which, after all, it assures it is fond—to
clear everything out of the way that can cause the Jews to convert
to Christianity out of impure and alien motives. The church can,
of course, not prescribe to the state either whether or under
which conditions it should allow Jews into the unlimited enjoyment of civil liberty. But it can declare before the whole world
that it has nothing at all against it; that it would in no way consider itself wounded if in this matter the state, without showing
the slightest consideration for religion, were to hit upon an
arrangement that agrees with its insights and intentions. The
church can beseechingly implore the state that if it does not wish
to set up any other way to accomplish this salutary change, it
might in the name of God also abolish the way things have been
done up to now, which brings it little advantage but bestows
untold harm upon the religious society; and let the state not
bestow any sort of civil right upon any Jew only because he has
converted to the church, either upon him or his children—since
the householders wanted to become Christians especially for the
sake of the children—or his grandchildren; for it is well known
that these are especially beloved and reared by the grandparents.
Indeed, it would scarcely be safe to permit the accomplished
change of religion to have a political influence, even in the fourth
generation; for if it is once taken to be virtuous to wound truth
for the sake of unknown advantage, such a virtuous hero might,
even in the fourth generation, easily take enough interest in
becoming a false Christian for the sake of this truth. To be sure,
this measure would still not suffice; this would only hold off
those who wanted to convert to Christianity to obtain rights; but
the number of those who take this step in order to be able to enter
into marital relations with Christians will surely be equally as
large. I would have something ready even for these.

It may perhaps not be advisable in most cases for a Christian
man and a Jewish woman (or vice versa) to contract a marriage
tie. But nothing actually stands written in the holy books about
its being unchristian and forbidden on account of religion.
Rather, the practice of the early church as well as all modern

churches, which are now being established among the gentiles, is very different from that in our Christian states. The church, which knows nothing about such a prohibition, would have to declare itself as follows: it would have no objections if the state were to abolish the law that exists for this purpose; it would even wish this to happen and subject itself in advance to all arrangements that the state was inclined to make in relation to such ties.[41] Certainly this heading would not remain as empty in the law books as the one regarding morganatic marriages.[42] Only through such declarations from every quarter can the Christian church cleanse itself from the suspicion that necessarily rests upon it under the present conditions and do its part to prevent the damage that threatens it. If the state does not want to listen, if the Jews do not want to reconcile themselves to anything else—which is quite possible—then things will proceed as heaven wishes, and we Christians can at least wash our hands in innocence.

This I also do now in relation to you in the event you still do not yet understand my interest in the matter and my opinion about it; and now I think you will have had enough.

Fourth Letter

P. . . , the 10th of May, 1799

No, I would not have expected to be so misunderstood by you. That I am an enemy of the Jews? That I believed secretly, perhaps even without knowing it, in their moral degradation? And all that merely because I did not want to have them in the Christian church! For all I care you can always draw conclusions from my remarks; I indeed intend to stand by them, if only you do them justice. Have you forgotten that I also wished the greatest portion of Christians were out of the church? Don't you reckon that almost all my good friends, even including you, are among

41. [Eds.] See *Gedanken* 1, Nr. 210: *KGA* I.2: 47,15–6: "The church requests the state to allow marriages, an act which is all the more appropriate, since it is seldom the case that the father is a Jew."

42. [Eds.] *Ehe zur linken Hand,* a marriage between unequals in which neither spouse nor children have inheritance rights.

them? And do you think that I also believe in your moral degradation? On this I will not defend myself further. So I fare, because I have the misfortune of being a Christian! Something like that is not taken for granted, and even those who know it think about it least just when they should do so. But I readily see that you have aimed at leading me further into the affair: you always play around with me when I engage in something with you, and afterwards reproach my prickly and polemical nature, and I simply haven't really learned yet. But this time your flash of wit will help you as little as your accusation.

Indeed, if I would have demanded something from the state, it would behoove me in such affairs, just as in economic matters, to have proposed a fund; but I only wish to repay the state its courtesies, and it will not be at a loss to know what to do with them. Or if it were at a loss, I might very easily point to respectable and secure places where it could invest them advantageously. Quite seriously, I in no way need to respond to your question regarding what kind of conditions the state should offer the Jews according to my idea and what they, for their part, should do. I actually only do so because I have already told you that and because you, of all people, ought to have found all this in my earlier formulations and because I would also like to laugh at you a little for the sake of this rarity. I have indeed admitted that the unlimited standing of ceremonial law is a political hindrance. I do not want them as Christians; yet if they should be citizens, about which I am perfectly serious, there are so many middle paths that you might fail to realize what I have in mind. This much I can say: I do not like the method of naturalization. If indeed a family that seeks this favorable status has such documents to declare,[43] as Mr. Friedländer has placed on record about a family that wanted this privilege,[44] this is then a completely

---

43. [Eds.] See *Gedanken* 1, Nr. 202; *KGA* I.2: 46,4–9: "The state may only demand from everyone the proofs, which the Fsche [sic] family (in Königsberg) gave when it petitioned for a letter of naturalization, namely that they had never been in a formal investigation, in a usury or a bankruptcy case, and had won in all civil suits an attestation on their relations with Christians, a recommendation from prominent men, and an assurance on account of education." That Schleiermacher recorded this incident in his early *Notebooks* indicates his degree of involvement with the issues at hand.

44. [Eds.] *Akten-Stücke* 48–51.

different political qualification than a baptismal certificate. But it is just too much; how would things stand if the state were to require so much from everyone? And it helps too little; for one will still always make difficulties in appointing a naturalized Jew to the courts, and in many other instances he would be terribly disadvantaged. In brief, I demand that the Jews who are serious about becoming citizens do not completely reject ceremonial law but only subordinate it to the laws of the state so that they would declare that they didn't want to escape from any civic duty under the pretext that it conflicts with ceremonial law. No one should be forbidden on account of religion from doing or undertaking anything that is allowed by the state. Further, I demand that they officially and publicly renounce the hope for a messiah; I believe this is an important point where the state cannot yield to them.

For a long time now the Jews have complained that, despite the fact that they have been born and raised in our part of the world for many centuries, the highest authorities always continue to treat them as foreigners, just as if they had first immigrated from Palestine.[45] Mr. Friedländer does this in his *Miscellaneous Documents, Concerning the Reform*,[46] but in the same book often refers to the Jews as a *nation*[47] and seems not to have noticed that this very expression completely justifies the state in its conduct. This is a matter that certainly belongs in your forum. Do you not find it completely natural and highly consistent that a state should not bestow full civil rights on persons who are driven from some other state only for some period of time? If French refugees[48] publicly declared completely openly that it was certain that they—sooner or later—would return to their fatherland, would the state not be perfectly authorized to view them immediately as foreigners, to exclude them from owning property and from assuming state offices, or to limit their activities in

45. [Eds.] See *Gedanken* 1, Nr. 203; *KGA* I.2: 46,10–2: "Friedländer in his *Miscellaneous Documents* [*Akten-Stücke*] always protests that the Jews should not be seen as foreign, and yet at times he himself calls them our nation."

46. [Eds.] *Akten-Stücke* 30–1.

47. [Eds.] *Akten-Stücke* 3, 5, 6, 26, 27, 30, 31, 33, 37.

48. [Eds.] Significant numbers of Protestant Huguenot refugees were in Prussia in the late eighteenth century and during the French revolution.

some other manner during their interim sojourn? And if they produced children and reared them in the same belief, and this were
to continue through many generations, would the mere length of
time be something that would have to move the state to change
its conduct, as long as the circumstances and convictions of these
guests remained the same? And regarding such convictions the
state can, after all, only judge from their formal utterances.

The Jews clearly find themselves in the same situation, as long
as the belief that at some time they will again be a proper nation
still defines their relation to one another and towards their fellow citizens and the state in a wholly distinctive manner. It may
be that this belief has few true followers any longer; but as long
as it remains a public confession, the state cannot treat them
other than by assuming that they believe in it, and thus it is not
to be blamed if it does not wish to bestow full civil rights upon
them. Just as one assumes that someone who leases a plot of
land for a couple of years and then intends to leave will spend
nothing on it and is apt to exhaust it, so it is also to be assumed
that those who do not view the state as their fatherland and as
their permanent home will also not concern themselves with
putting forth their best effort but only wish to draw the best possible advantage from it, even if to its ruin. If there should be any
truth in all that is said about the political crimes of the Jews, it
derives from this source. Only for this reason, to the disadvantage of the state, do they cling to their ceremonial laws, because
these are the laws of their actual fatherland; only for this reason
can one with certain plausibility accuse the lower class among
them of a greater inclination to deception, because the sense of
justice of all uneducated persons is only juridical and not moral
and thus cannot be so pure in relation to persons with whom
they believe themselves to be in relationship only for a short
time, and who are only in it unhappily.

Who would wish to deny that our own common people are
well inclined to deceive foreigners? Only for this reason do the
Jews separate themselves from other fellow citizens, so that when
the time of departure comes, they may be as little entangled as
possible while being bound together as much as possible. Even
the exclusive predilection for commerce and, as soon as it was
invented, trading in money, for which Jews are reproached, and
the ease with which they have so long endured being held within

these bounds by the laws, can be traced back to these factors, since these occupations are least tied to the earth, and facilitate quite well the swift transplantation of one's entire property into distant regions.

Finally, I demand that those who accept both points[49] should constitute a special ecclesiastical society. The state must be sure that the change of religion that it declares necessary is always connected with the advantages that it bestows. If those who have embraced this altered Judaism remain mingled with the rest and distinguish themselves through nothing but the provisional act of their confession, the state loses them from view and cannot know what kind of change occurs in their convictions, or at least those of their progeny, due to family circumstances or foreign education.

Thus the state cannot attach unconditionally the propagation of granted civil advantages to the descendants, any more than it can get involved with specifically demanding this declaration from each individual, perhaps at coming-of-age, since the state generally does not renew a civil contract specifically with each individual. Thus I know of no other means than that the community of those who have laid down this confession constitute a special moral person on whom the particular civil advantages shall be bestowed, so that the advantages will be acquired upon entrance into the same and forfeited with voluntary separation—for you can trust me not to institute the right of the ban. Be amused if you will, I am completely serious about this new sect.

And this, you will say, I was supposed to have surmised from your earlier utterances? Indeed! But surely no one but you will say this, who thought that I denigrate the *Open Letter* excessively and polemicize against it with all my powers. What then do I have against it? I have shown that it is full of the spirit of Judaism and of love for the same and that the conversion to Christianity is a false deed that does not belong in it. For the remainder, I must thus, in accord with your assumption, be in agreement, for otherwise I would have contested much more; and what remains is

49. [Eds.] The preceding conditions (subordination of ceremonial law to Prussian civil law, renouncing the hope for a messiah) are here joined by a call to establish a proto-Reform Jewish sect that would receive official state recognition.

exactly all that which I have now demanded, for actually the author strives for these things in the same spirit.[50] He wants to put aside the ceremonial law, but the manner in which he determines the lawfulness of this action already proves that he means this only so far as is suited and necessary to fit the times; from that point he is only driven into Christianity by his evil demon, by a false tendency; he recognizes the need for a religious society, because the "eternal truths"[51] otherwise do not survive, yet for this reason he sees these eternal truths as deriving from Judaism as a positive religion and belonging to it. Of course, he thinks of this religious society as a "middle thing between Jews and Christians,"[52] but according to his way of thinking not unjustly; for if one in accord with law has to destroy the law for the sake of the eternal, one still remains under the law, i.e., in Judaism. Finally, he presents belief in the messiah as an accidental doctrine that actually only derives from misunderstanding.[53] Thus once one has wholly excluded its false elements, the *Open Letter* contains everything that the state can demand from the Jews and is the true codex of a new Judaism, capable and worthy of political existence in every respect.

You see how little I am against the *Open Letter* when I allot it this place! I see the *Task* and the *Open Letter* as necessary and complementary pieces and believe that, taken together, both contain everything that the Jews have to do for their benefit: the former indirectly by provoking the state to depart from its accustomed way; the latter directly by opening a new way to it. And I would further like to know, and wish you would tell me, what valid objections the state can still make against those who have declared and constituted themselves this way and what could keep the state from bestowing everything on them with which it makes its other children happy. Under *valid* objections I would, however, include all those things that do not solely refer to abuses, whose abolition the state itself should already have considered. Accept the challenge, if you still have hesitations in the matter, and let me hear from you.

50. [Eds.] See *OL*, 67; *Sendschreiben* 58–60; *KGA* I.2: 402,23–403,15.
51. [Eds.] See *OL*, 78; *Sendschreiben* 84: *KGA* I.2: 412,22.
52. [Eds.] See *OL*, 77; *Sendschreiben* 84; *KGA* I.2: 412,15.
53. [Eds.] See *OL*, 58–60; *Sendschreiben* 38–43; *KGA* I.2: 395,9–397,2.

Fifth Letter

P. . . , the 19th of May, 1799

It wasn't exactly gallant of you not to accept the challenge of getting mixed up with those details that I have against me, but it is truly noble to have declined doing battle with a political novice. You are not eager to find out, at this opportunity, all the things I take to be abuses? That would not be so bad, I assure you; but, as you say, it is more comfortable for you to put me to flight because of my manner of generalities. Except that *your* manner seems, successfully, to have taken over *my* manner. For of this I assure you: the Westphalian Peace remains something much too specialized for me; when you talk about it like a state counselor,[54] I am immediately silenced, because I do not understand the slightest thing about it and do not at this point still have the least desire to make its acquaintance. In my *naiveté* I could say I thought it would work more against a new Christian sect than against a Jewish one.

But what does this concern me? And what does it have to do with the whole matter? If the Westphalian Peace has had such a good constitution as to be able to swallow all the pills up to now without dying of them, then it will probably also endure this. And where exactly is its seat? In Wetzlar and Regensburg it indeed rules strongly,[55] but its arm doesn't seem to reach much further. The result of this is that the king could not name such a Jew to be a delegate[56] or present him to the Imperial Court, but I should think that these honors might easily be dispensed with.

What you say about the unworkability of such a separation in regard to the state is surely not meant seriously and goes too much in circles. A Judaism without the evil because of which the state does not want Judaism can scarcely be held to be a new evil; it also can't bother the state with something new of its own, except if one proceeds on the assumption that Jews, nevertheless, in the end should become Christians. In regard to the Jews, allow

54. [Eds.] *Kabinetsrath.*

55. [Eds.] Wetzlar had been the seat of the Imperial Court (*Reichskammergericht*) since 1693; Regensburg, the meeting site of the Permanent Imperial Diet of the Old Empire (*Immerwährender Reichstag des Alten Reiches*) since 1663.

56. [Eds.] *Comitialgesandte.*

us to take the situation as it actually is and can't otherwise be. As soon as a portion of a greater mass takes form in a special and particular manner, this portion strives to separate from the latter and to attain an independent existence: this is an eternal law of nature, and I don't see how Jews might escape it. Educated Jews are surely well aware of the sharp distinction that exists between them and the rest; the separation has in fact existed a long time, and it is most unseemly for it not to be constituted externally.

The better Jews have created for themselves a very good and praiseworthy principle that obliges them to have an effect on the rest and to do more for them than for themselves; and this principle stands wholly against the effort to seek a path into Christianity. It is clear not only that not all would take this path but also that the bitterness of those staying behind toward those who left would be so strong that all those who are somewhat serious about their religion will have less in common with these converts than with older Christians. The richer orthodox Jews—and such persons probably exist—will completely take sides with the lower class, with all its superstitions and bad characteristics, and would certainly by their influence support hatred of Christians and the fatherland far more strongly than is the case up to now. The more those branches of commerce practiced by those Jews who have become Christians might be given up for other occupations, the more the orthodox Jews will concentrate in branches of commerce, and the riches, which are connected to the uncultivated class, will become all the greater, a thing that is undeniably a great evil. In this manner every good effect of better persons on others is ended, and the uneducated must remain alone, armed threefold against everything that might be undertaken for their betterment.

But just as little do I believe that the Christianized Jews will accomplish something if they remain connected to the orthodox Jews in their accustomed manner. What have they thereby won up to now? Nothing, except to sacrifice themselves in a useless manner. If at times of reform the government would have dealt with a select group of the Jewish nation,[57] as would arise through my proposal, something salutary certainly would have occurred at that time, at least for these persons; but those who wished to purchase improvement even through some religious self-sacrifices

---

57. [Eds.] See *Gedanken* 1, Nr. 206 and 208; *KGA* I.2: 47,4–6 and 10–1.

did not want to separate from those who hung on to the strict letter of the law; rather they hoped that these would be drawn over
to the better side by a charitable authoritative decree with a gentle
use of power, a plan that failed due to the government's liberality
and conscientiousness. You will, without doubt, easily recall the
passages in the *Miscellaneous Documents,* which I here have in
mind.[58] Even with the most untainted honesty one incurs all too
easily such minor transgressions against strict legality when one
begins to oppose the indications of nature. These clearly seem to
me to move toward such a separation, as I have taken them to be
the true tendency of the one party based on the writing of its
spokesman, and I believe that the influence of this party on the
others is not thereby lost but established all the more.

As long as the better persons are completely mixed together
with the others, they can always only work individually and not
as a body with united powers; they cannot even (owing to considerations that they have to take into account in order not to give
offence) represent their convictions openly. Only then, when they
achieve their own critical mass and don't appear to want to have
any effect on the others, can their example have an effect; their
conviction can then show itself freely and on a large scale; and
the moral and civil advantages, which are accorded to them, are
not only a matter of aspiration but actually perceived. It is also
not to be expected that the more orthodox part of the nation
would be as embittered by this change of things as by the conversion to Christianity, for it cannot escape them that the law is
revered by them[59] and the essence of Judaism preserved; similarly, the distinction will also not be so sharp that transition
should not be very easy. Since the ceremonial law is not wholly
cast aside but is only to be limited, and thus persons belonging to
the emancipated Jews can honor and observe it to some considerable degree, the less strict among those who remain behind will
always be able to find persons among the emancipated Jews
whose orthodoxy is not very different from their own.

You think that if I just didn't want to pay heed to the difficulties that only arise out of old wounds and deficiencies in our constitution, it would seem to you that an association similar to the

58. [Eds.] Cf. *Akten-Stücke* 88–100, 129–35, 170–83.

59. [Eds.] By the new group of emancipated Jews.

New East-Prussian Regulation would be preferable in every respect to such a split. I do not wish to respond to that in detail. In applying this to our German lands there would be little similarity remaining, and even less would be achieved towards that which our German Jews want and what I as a Christian have wished for them. I appeal directly to you yourself, who will very soon discover that. Otherwise you do indeed know how much I have delighted in this regulation; in this matter it can produce much good, though to be sure only as a provisional constitution, if only it were now to commence, be followed, and implemented.

Sixth Letter

P. . . , the 30th of May, 1799

Mercy, my dear friend, what all have you sent me as punishment for my sins? What a flood of vulgarities, if this word isn't itself too noble. I suppose I shouldn't be surprised that this sort of thing has been written with respect to this matter. It would be unreasonable if in a city like Berlin there were not an enormous number of whining scribblers, and wherever fifty of my clerical brothers come together, it seems to me wholly natural that one of them should be of this ilk.[60] The topic is especially provocative for these people, and they have—this much one must grant them— done their part to amuse themselves in their own way about the matter. But that *nothing else* than this has come to the surface has disturbed me to no little extent. Has no proper person who has real ideas and knows how to speak reasonably with reasonable people taken enough interest in the affair to utter a word about it? Concerning a matter that lies at the heart of our practical life?

In fact, I now no longer know what I am to think about Berlin scholars! I have always viewed them as social people and businessmen and have thus not been surprised about their total silence in fields that are speculative; but that they have nothing to say about a matter like this, which in just these features would

---

60. [Eds.] A probable allusion to the anonymous pamphlet *An einige Hausväter jüdischer Religion, über die vorgeschlagene Verbindung mit den protestantischen Christen. Von einem Prediger in Berlin* (2 Hefte: Berlin, 1799); the author appears to be unknown, *KGA* I.2: 359n.

have to touch them in many ways, I can understand all the less, since otherwise they do not at all neglect the topic of occasional papers and often have taken the first opportunity to be able to compose one. And they are surely not incredulous about the utility of writing in general, since everything of that sort that comes to us and is truly Berlin-ish is calculated for its utility. It must, then, be a pure lack of interest just in this affair. Now, to be sure, insofar as it has some relation to religion and inasmuch as the talk should turn to Christianity in some sort of fashion, this is wholly in order! But there is supposed to be a fair amount of association in Berlin between Christians and Jews, especially among scholars, and that even this personal interest has not been able to prevail over the former consideration is a truly remarkable act of abstention. At its core I am inclined to conclude that the sentiment in Berlin may be rather widespread. That seems to be the case in the most honest of the pieces that have appeared: that, for example, one must take a rather broad view of the truth[61] wherever genuine moral utility can be achieved,[62] that everything positive is only cultus[63]—a suitably fabricated word—and religion is everywhere the same, and that it is thus nothing but an affectation when Jews, out of alleged conscientiousness, either don't wish to become Christians at all, or only in a certain manner.[64] Others may have thus been quietly delighted about an imminent Christianity without Christ, and yet they still do not wish to breathe a word about the thing, which, for their own sake, they rightly do. But I would have hoped that from the side of the Berlin clergy something might have happened to make good what that Mr. Clerical Brother has spoilt. I am ashamed when I think it is possible that worthy Jews, who, however, know so few clergy and hardly have a proper idea of this class of persons, might draw inferences about the others from this one. Reassure me about this if at all possible. If you are only able to assure me that the greater part of the Berlin clergy conduct themselves as they ought to do in this matter, that without hesitation they—

61. [Eds.] Cf. *Beantwortung des an Herrn Probst Teller erlassenen Sendschreibens einigter Hausväter jüdischer Nation. Nicht von Teller,* especially 20–2.

62. [Eds.] *Beantwortung. . . Nicht von Teller,* 13–6.

63. [Eds.] *Beantwortung. . . Nicht von Teller,* 31, 36–7, yet see also 28–9.

64. [Eds.] *Beantwortung. . . Nicht von Teller,* 13, 16–7, 19–20, 30–1, 41–2.

as men and as members of the literary world—also close ranks with those who do not shy away from association with educated and learned Jews, and that in everything that belongs to social life they take no notice of this separation of religions; then I will happily forgive their silence, for action is better than speaking.

Mr. Teller's response is for me an agreeable sign that the revered and, in fact, amiable man is again recovering from his ailing condition and has also otherwise delighted me. Instructively and benevolently he dwells upon the circumstances of the document directed at him, and his response also gives several significant suggestions. Without hesitation he presents his private opinion to an audience with which he has such diverse relationships, and with rare resignation he casts aside all worldly considerations in order to clarify, according to his insight, only that about which he's been asked. It's good that you, at least, haven't held back this response, since with its help I have had to recover for the rest of the debate.

Wilhelm Abraham Teller:
Response to the Open Letter to Me, Provost Teller, from Some Householders of the Jewish Religion[1]

Christ:
It is the spirit that gives life; the flesh is useless.
The words that I have spoken to you are spirit and life.
Gospel of John 6:63

Esteemed Sirs!
Very worthy Friends!

If you need to be equally respectful of every reader of your *Open Letter* to me as you are to me considering your reverence toward God and conscience as well as your love of truth and virtue deeply expressed therein, so the good will and confidence particularly attested to me thereby oblige me just as publicly to assure you, as friends, of my honest high esteem.

As the only possible expression of this that I can make in relation to unknown persons, accept then the following response. I have thereby intentionally repressed the wish that it might please you, so as not to allow any influence on the free presentation of my views and convictions. But now, since this presentation is completed, I heartily wish that through our published exchange of letters in such an extremely important matter, as far as it is known in Christian lands, at least a good seed might be dispersed that gradually sprouts in a favorable political climate and bears fruit toward the recognition of the same essential human dignity of your brethren. May this fruit also be considered ripe by the Most High, who looks down with the same enjoyment on all his true devotees.

I proceed immediately with something that for me is, admittedly, only a secondary matter but unusually worthy of increasing

1. Wilhelm Abraham Teller, *Beantwortung des Sendschreibens einiger Hausväter jüdischer Religion an mich den Probst Teller* (Berlin: August Mylius, 1799).

recognition and proper evaluation by all Christians and non-Christians who live alongside one another in accord with their external confession.

Here I am taking into account what you, esteemed sirs, have noted incidentally in your *Open Letter* about the unsuitability of your nation's never fully developed original language for expressing intellectual concepts; about its wholly natural decline in culture amid such diverse sad fates; finally, about the immorality that is wrongly imputed to the nation. Certainly all of that is very true and well expressed. Even those of our linguistic scholars who are actually worthy of this name agree with you in respect to the first matter. Besides the examples adduced by you, it is said about every talented man—about the construction expert as well as about the prophet—that the *spirit of God is in him,* without in the least expressing at the same time the greater efficacy of the spirit in the prophet. For were this to occur, one could very likely ascribe such a thing to religiosity, which happily traces back everything noble and good in man to God as its original source. Likewise, there is only a scant knowledge of history involved, as far as the aforementioned deep decay of the nation is concerned, from which moral corruption was an almost inevitable consequence.

And so every attentive observer of mankind will consider himself convinced that as concerns morality, no people, viewed as a whole, as yet has any advantage over another people; that presently in Christian cities and lands there prevail often greater, though in part only more refined, vices and misdeeds than among heathens; and that even the transgressions for which they are chastised as more typical for persons of the synagogue are caused by the pressure of their circumstances. To be sure, these permit no justification but still deserve fair, sympathetic excuses. In brief: Paul's utterance, "*they are all sinners,*"[2] where he speaks about the moral corruption of mankind, taken as a whole among Hebrews and Greeks, barbarians and Romans, will retain its validity as long as among a majority of religious parties mere external worship of God is mistaken for actual religiosity, as long as reverence for God is considered merely as a matter of memorization—but not an affair of the heart and life—and as already dealt with in early instruction. Paul's utterance will retain its

2. Romans 3:23

validity as long as wisdom—which reigns at the side of the Most High and whose rays, even when they are only refracted, God lets fall on our darkened earthly life in order to bless it and to prepare us for that brighter light that would only blind us in present circumstances—as long as this wisdom, I say, is degraded to a cold, dry science and its illuminating rays, which encourage enthusiasm for every virtue, cannot penetrate the fog of dark questions and those clouds of dust stirred up and intensified by those makers of system who fight against each other.

In all of that we are thus in agreement. And so I am also fully of your opinion in what you especially assert about the spirit and wisdom of the lawgiver Moses, according to which the entire ceremonial practices, over time and under other circumstances, are supposed to fall away of their own accord. At the same time, it is also certainly a very astute and penetrating view of this practice when you assume that the bulk of the customs prescribed thereby—which continually engage eyes, hands, and all senses and yet which all bear upon the one God, creator and ruler of the universe—has been, however, the only means of preservation for a people that is confounded by a long suppression and inclined to the service of idols. This indeed is the happiest resolution of a very difficult task, as you call it, whereby Moses appears in a very brilliant light. It is altogether truly annoying when the old and recent [champions of Thomas] Paine[3] among the French, from time immemorial—if not more ignorant then more foolish than

3. [Eds.] Teller alludes to the impact of the radical revolutionary and outspoken deist within the American and the French revolutions. Born a Quaker in England, Thomas Paine (1737–1809) wrote *Common Sense* (1776), which became the most famous pamphlet calling for American independence from England. In England after 1787, he championed the French revolution against Edmund Burke in his *Rights of Man* (1791) and then moved to Paris, where he was lionized by the French and made an honorary citizen, and where his works were widely translated. Thomas Paine, *Kurzer Abriß der Entstehung der französischen Revolution* (Leipzig: Dyk, 1791); *Über die Regierungen und die Ur-Grundsätze einer jeden derselben* (Paris, 1794). While in prison in Paris, he wrote *Age of Reason: Being an Investigation of True and Fabulous Theology* (1794; German tr. Paris, 1796 [New York: Willey Book Company, 1940]), which offers a notoriously critical view of the Bible, revelation, and supernaturalism. In addition to arguing against the Mosaic authorship of the Bible, Paine denounces the bloodthirsty passages of the Bible and adds that "the character of Moses, as stated in the Bible, is the most horrid that can be imagined. If those accounts be true, he was the wretch that first began

those of England—pass over everything that relates to the story of Moses. Let them at least rightly consider—which in any case requires the least presence of mind—his measures as military leader of such a great crowd of people with respect to preserving order and purity in the camp and installing the tabernacle as its headquarters and as its advance unit while marching, measures taken to show the army the way in an immense wilderness by steam and smoke in the day and by fire at night, and so forth. Yet I mention this only in passing.

One could now, to be sure, still counter your special presentation of Moses' two intended purposes for ceremonial practices by saying: "He should not have burdened the Israelites with them, that thereby their spirit is now crushed rather than elevated, and it has been made nearly impossible for them to pull themselves together for a more worthy, nobler worship of God." But to that I would now respond: that he, indeed, had considered even this disadvantageous result as easily possible, included it in his plans, yet also guarded against it. Namely so: he made known the basic law of the Ten Commandments as directly written by God himself,[4] yet all ceremonial and ritual laws as only sketched by him and, as it were, dictated to him. Indeed, the former were engraved on stone tablets as valid through all epochs, and the latter were merely written in transitory script—the former, finally, only under the awesome signs of the nearness of God. Yes, one could even conjecture that these ten commandments, after the destruction of the two tablets,[5] would have been written down by Moses only as a reminder that even this still very imperfect moral law will in time yield to a more perfect one and make the *scriptural* admonition of the former unnecessary, which Jeremiah and the author of the Letter to the Hebrews also suggested.[6]

Accordingly, the system of ceremonies was an actual slavery for people who were not yet capable of a freer and more spontaneous worship of God. It was the first training of underage children

---

and carried on wars on the score or on the pretence of religion; and under that mask, or that infatuation, committed the most unexampled atrocities that are to be found in the history of any nation. . . . " (118–9).

4. Exodus 24:12; 32:16.

5. Exodus 34:27–8.

6. Jeremiah 31:33; Hebrews 8:10.

who could not be reared differently. This stands in comparison to the treatment of those who are already able to use their reason more and listen sooner to fatherly reprimands and admonitions. In *content* and *composition* even the Ten Commandments were more civil laws—of a governmental constitution in which God himself was alone the direct ruler—than moral prescriptions. Even if the Israelite followed them meticulously, which still hardly made him a truly God-fearing and thoughtful man, he was in this respect only a lawful citizen. Thus the first three of the first tablet (according to the original manner of dividing and enumerating them): "You shall have no other gods before me; you shall not make images," and so forth; "you shall not take the name of God in vain," were only strictly prohibitive. The same is true of the five of the second tablet; in the first case prohibiting high treason against the ruler and in the second case every offence against a fellow citizen's life—his marital relationship, his possessions, his good name before the court, as well as his entire domestic state.

Consequently, all are nothing but such rank offenses that would very soon give the deathblow to any state, especially in its first beginnings. Neither was the actual worship of the only true God specified in the first three, nor was some kind of proper conviction *demanded* in the last five. The fourth, about *celebrating the Sabbath* in a really commanding tone, was more a police regulation for the preservation of health and even the physical powers of useful household animals, such as any ruler could give for the betterment of the state. Originally, as is best known to you, much-honored friends, there was no worship service connected with rendering the seventh day holy, such as with us in the celebration of Sunday. Only later was the reading of scripture added in Jewish synagogues, and whatever one of their teachers wished to say by way of edification at its instance. However, this commandment immediately followed on those that directly concerned the political sovereignty, to avail myself of this expression, since it was supposed to be followed in imitation of the daily work the Israelites' ultimate superior completed on the sixth day, as Creator of the world.

Finally, the fifth—or, as we count, fourth, similarly commanding, and recorded on the first tablet—assumed this place in the middle between the preceding and the following, because it makes a transition from a central duty in domestic society to those duties to their fellow citizens in the public sphere. It also has this middle position since parents are to be considered as the subordinate authorities of their house and children are accustomed to rapt obedience towards them. Also, subsequently, with their entrance into the larger society, the children will so much more easily carry over this obedience to their superiors and even to the highest national sovereign. This middle position is also apt, as the Jewish writer Philo explains,[7] because parents are, as it were, the subordinate creators of their children.

Hence these ten commandments, apart from that about the Sabbath, are of permanent validity; but it is well to note this fact, not insofar as they contained the first instruction for the Israelites, which was only intended to curb the externally crudest immoral conduct, but because they are self-evident when the human being has already been trained for higher morality. The Ten Commandments are the ABCs of this morality or of the *law written on everyone's heart*, from which letters all precepts are gradually expressed through written signs of it. All instructions for correctly held convictions should be compiled and get admitted to the general knowledge of true worshipers of God without distinguishing between country or people; they should be made known to them for the same adherence.

If I, moreover, still exempt the commandment to rest on the seventh day from this eternal validity, this comes to pass because it does not, like the rest, concern a civil law of rights and duties but must be considered as a mere police regulation. That is what the sublime founder of the Christian religion meant when he rejected the Pharisees' reproach of his disciples on account of their alleged illegal conduct on the Sabbath with the remark: "The Sabbath is made for man, not man for the Sabbath."[8] On this idea he based the so-fitting response to the question put before him by the same Pharisees, so incriminating in their judgment or their intent; "Is it proper to heal on the Sabbath?": "If an ox or an ass falls into a well, will you not pull it out on the day of the Sabbath"?[9] They could only counter it with their private indignation

---

7. In the *Treatise about Ten Commandments*.
8. Mark 2:27.
9. Luke 14:3; cf. Matthew 12:10 and John 7:22–3.

at not being able to reply to it. They could have drawn this con-
clusion for themselves in an honest manner or unblinded by the
hairsplitting of Talmudic scholars: if the law even offers remis-
sion from the usual work for cattle, of what use could this remis-
sion be to the animal if you did not want to save its life on the
Sabbath and preferred this duty of duties itself, to rest from your
daily work? On this basis, the first Christians could continue for a
long while to celebrate the Sabbath as a day of rest but also, later,
choose a different universal day of rest. And so our celebration of
Sunday is itself, to be sure, a very salutary police regulation, since
Christian rulers after Constantine the Great have confirmed it;
but it is in no way an essential requirement of the religion, as
Luther very correctly observed in his Greater Catechism.

In order to come closer now to what for me is the main issue of
this response: Even you—distinguishing yourselves so brilliantly
in your[10] letter as very correctly thinking and, what is even more
valid, maturely reflecting men—are convinced that all Mosaic
statutory laws should have been only preliminary steps toward
actual religion and morality; that your nation should have long
since passed from the age of childhood into the adult age of reason; and that, accordingly, since its training for this is complete,
you are not further obliged to those laws yet are indeed obliged to
acknowledge the eternal truths of reason that underlie the true
dignity of humanity. And how should that have not already long
since happened with your whole nation? It was the case that wise
men and prophets, one after another, called out to them with such
a loud and unified voice: *"God doesn't require sacrifices and gifts"* (as
if he had never prescribed them); *"doing right and good are dearer to
him than sacrifice; he takes delight in love and not sacrifice"* (after they
had made these sacrifices long enough); *"the sacrifice that would
please him would be an anxious spirit and a broken,"* repentant heart
that is inclined toward improving one's mind.[11]

How could their forefathers turn a deaf ear to their so excel-
lently named preacher, Solomon, and his strong as well as true
remark: "Preserve your foot when you go to the house of God,
and come that you might hear! *That is better than the sacrifice of
fools;* for since they cannot help being that, they do not *know* or

10. [Eds.] Taking *Ihren* for *ihren*.
11. Wisdom of Solomon 21:3; 1 Samuel 15:22; Hosea 6:6, Psalms 51:19.

consider what *they do*."[12] How could they misunderstand Isaiah in
the slightest way when he had raised the voice of God against all
chastisements of the body? Should that be a fast I *choose*, which I
approve, it shall give me enjoyment and, as it were, I shall be
indemnified for all your offenses against my eternal law, that a
man may harm his body, and so forth. That is a fast I choose: let
go those whom you imprison with injustice; leave untrammeled
what you have burdened down; leave free those whom you
oppress; break your bread for the hungry, and so forth.[13] How
could they, finally, have left unnoticed the long, splendid description of the pious man who is to be excluded from the common
misery, which description is lacking any consideration of a fast, a
gift, a sacrifice? Here in Ezekiel[14] the proverbial question in the
second verse, to which this is the answer, intends to say as much:
"The forefathers sowed it and the descendants have to reap it."

Yet even I gladly excuse them, your earlier ancestors, even
though the majority of them defiantly rejected the head of the
Christian community, crowned with glory and honor, despite his
death on the cross. The priests, the priests—not a Gamaliel[15] of
that confused era, from whose school later Paul, indisputably the
most brilliant among the apostles, came forth—the priests were at
fault. They misled the masses, which are alike among all religious
confessions and find a material cultus most comfortable for themselves, whereby they need no independent reflection, no real giving up of their earthly understanding, and which cultus rather
only deadens them more and more to both. In addition to that,
your casuists came later, the subsequently so-called *Talmudists*, who
now wholly confused minds with their endless legal questions
and decisions, so that up to the times of Christ the nation no
longer relished a Sirach[16] and other moral writers; and presum-
ably for this reason, they let the Hebrew original of Sirach get lost.

Thus it is then—after so many a century, an appearance as
unexpected as illuminating, equal only to a not-yet-calculated

12. Ecclesiastes 5:1 [adapted].

13. Isaiah 58:5–7 [paraphrase].

14. Ezekiel 18:3–9 [responding to 18:2].

15. [Eds.] Acts 5:34, 22:3.

16. [Eds.] As a book in the Old Testament apocrypha, Sirach arose during the
Hellenistic period of the rise of Judaism; hence it is a Greek text.

comet in the churchly heaven, which precisely makes you, too, especially venerable to me—that you renounce the ceremonial duties of your ancestral law as no longer binding for you in its first intent. It is really a heartening step that you take and which, we surely hope to God, will have some kind of beneficial consequence, whatever might become of your Protestantism. Even you yourselves have recognized it, with thanks in your letter that you live in such a land and under such a government, and that altogether times and circumstances have gone before which make it easier for you to be able to take this step with all circumspection. Even this noble wisdom of religion, like everything in the nature of things, is a daughter of time. First, more than thirty years ago, the wise Moses Mendelssohn had to stand up among you and, in social intercourse as through writing and virtuous conduct, awaken the moral sense of your fellow believers; first your Friedländer had to come forth from his school; famous physicians,[17] like Bloch, Herz, and Davidson among us and others in larger and smaller cities of the Prussian monarchy, won the trust of the most prominent Christian families not only through their art but also through other sciences and genuine philosophies of humanity, which destroyed much superstition. For example, the science of Professor Herz[18] destroyed the superstition about early burials, making himself of value and important in the greater public; your Euchel[19] wrote the moral *sampler;* your Lazarus Bendavid[20] pursued the first of all sciences. Even Protestant theologians had to be more inclined to recognize their accomplishments

17. [Eds.] See John M. Efron, *Medicine and the German Jews: A History,* Ch. 3, "*Haskalah* and Healing: Jewish Medicine in the Age of Enlightenment" (New Haven: Yale University Press, 2001) 64–104.

18. [Eds.] An allusion to *Über die frühe Beerdigung der Juden* (Berlin, 1788) by Marcus Herz (1747–1803), in which the prominent Berlin physician and leading student of Kant advocated postponing burial for seventy-two hours to avoid burying someone alive; in his day the custom among Berlin Jews was to bury within four hours. See Efron, *Medicine and the German Jews* 92–104.

19. [Eds.] Isaac Abraham Euchel (1758–1804), studied philosophy under Kant, perfected his Hebrew under Moses Mendelssohn and Naphtali Wessely, and was a founder of the Hebrew language journal of Enlightened Jewry, *Ha-meassef* (1783).

20. [Eds.] Lazarus Bendavid (1762–1832), a staunch adherent of Kant, studied at Göttingen and Halle and served as director of the Berlin *Freischule* (Jewish Free School), founded by David Friedländer and Daniel Itzig, from 1806–25.

impartially. Finally, even in social intercourse your fellow believers are becoming more intermingled with ours; their outward customs and the entire way of life are more similar to ours, so that even through this association many an idea that otherwise remained foreign to you worked unnoticed upon you as the transition to others related to it. All of that, I say, had to precede in order to prepare the way for you, too, honored friends, to prepare the way for your views now declared in print.

I thus take heartfelt delight in your giving up a mere legal training of servants, but only for so long a time until these can be elevated to the freedom of children of God, and wish that you might find more and more followers. Of course, there were already very early among your forefathers the so-called Essenes or Essaer, whose worship of God consisted solely of a contemplative life, a simple manner of life without any Mosaic practices. To be sure, Pliny in the *Natural History*[21] seems to fix their age much too high and also may have exaggerated their complete celibacy only in order to be able to adduce the play of words, "a people lasting an eternity through the centuries without any procreation of children, because all who are tired of the life and the reeling around in the vast society turn to them." Thus it is nonetheless certain from the corroborative documents of Josephus in *Jewish Antiquities*,[22] of Philo in the work, *On the Virtuous as the Only Free Man*, and of Porphyry, *On Moderation*, that they already constituted a third Jewish religious party alongside the Pharisees and Sadducees in Judea where it borders on Syria. Dwelling especially in this place, they lived an ascetic life, ascribed a greater sanctity to celibacy, lived mostly in villages and pursued agriculture, conjecturally even disappeared with the rise of monasticism among Christians. What had made them especially notable to Christian scholars does not belong here. I only wanted to say that, even though good men, they were, even more than that, enthusiasts who had too high-flown ideas about a sacred sensibility and conduct. Indeed, they were the *most honorable*, as Porphyry names them in his language, in comparison with the other two parties, but even still too illiberal, foregoing the cheerful enjoyment of life and exhibiting a merit-seeking mental deficiency in small ways,

21. In the fifteenth chapter of the fifth book.
22. 18, 1.

such as wearing white clothing, going barefoot, and the like. By contrast, you, highly respected friends, are now serious thinkers in this and about that which is the most important affair of mankind: "to honor and love God and be well-disposed in accord with his holy law."[23]

But now I wish to ask you, not as Christian theologian, but as the friend of an affair that is also good and desirable, why you do not rest satisfied with having separated the pure gold of your original Israelite confession from the ignoble aspects that were added to it later? Already then, when Lavater issued the well-known rash demand to convert to Moses Mendelssohn of blessed memory, I did not in the least way, alongside several others of colder reflection, wish that he might heed it.[24] Now, my stance, to be sure, initially surprised, among others, a certain Mr. v. H——g from the H——schen, to whom I uttered this when I met him in Bad Lauchstädt. But he soon recovered from this shock when I explained myself regarding the matter as follows. In the first place, I said Mendelssohn would immediately lose all influence among his fellow believers, for whose improvement of moral convictions he takes such pains with so much spirit and energy. I asked whether it is not desirable that he could therein be effective for the longest time possible in order to bring them closer to the time when, in Paul's judgment, *all Israel will be saved* and, as this is to be understood, will join in the Christian fold.[25] In the second place this would also have been the opinion of Christ in a very similar case: "Do not hinder him," (one who does such a great work), *even if he is not immediately among my followers;* "for whoever is not against us is for us;"[26] whoever works with us towards the same ends thereby already declares himself to be for us. Is this not also spoken for all times as true as it is excellent and so worthy of consideration for all conversion-seeking followers in

23. [Eds.] Teller's summary of the meaning of the religion of the Old Testament.
24. [Eds.] An allusion to the young Zürich theologian Johann Casper Lavater (1741–1801), who, recognizing Mendelssohn's keen intelligence and religious sensitivity, challenged him to convert to Christianity. *German-Jewish History in Modern Times,* vol. 1, ed. Michael A. Meyer (New York: Columbia University Press, 1996), 280, 336–7.
25. Romans 11:26.
26. Luke 9:50.

all churches? It is also still apt to observe—parenthetically but nonetheless really without an intended insult—that even the otherwise so gentle John, whose person is supposed to amble about again in Mr. *Lavater,* on this occasion played the intolerant one.

Hence you, esteemed ones, already have Christ's mind to this extent. Why now would you also want the ecclesiastical standing of those who are called by his name? Does not the well-considered disposition bestow its own worth sufficiently before all right-minded Christians, before your conscience and before the One who knows our heart and who only judges us accordingly and sets us right? Will you not thereby lose all effective power over the mass of your local and foreign brethren to the same convictions of a more genuine and more reasonable religiosity? Who is able to decide whether it is not the plan of the Eternal One to use you to that end? Whether it is not included in the same plan for you and for your strength of mind, for the sake of so good a deed, even provisionally to do without the standing of the external church in Christian states? Indeed, on page 77 you fear that without the public step you wish to be able to take, your principles, in the few families where they are at home, might scarcely keep alive and might again die out with them.[27] To this I answer you with the pious singer: "The race of the pious will be blessed—its righteousness remains eternally—*it will never more be forgotten.*"[28] Therewith will the memory of its manner of thought and mind, devoted to God in spirit and truth, also endure and continue to have an effect.

Yet when you now, with laudable frankness, confess on page 77 the intention of immediately requiring the rights of a citizen with your entrance into the community of Christians, I indeed have to leave aside the question of what a Christian state might further demand from you for the bestowal of this right when you have once given up the ceremonial law. I only understand so much, that a great hindrance nevertheless thereby falls away, which until now had made your fellow believers unacceptable to incorporation among other citizens. It hasn't even been so long

27. [Eds.] See especially *Open Letter* (hereafter *OL*) 77: "We shall answer these questions frankly. . . ." Here, and elsewhere, when Teller makes direct reference to Friedländer's *Open Letter,* page references are transposed to the present edition.

28. Psalms 112:2, 3, 6.

since I found the following relevant passage, here literally translated by me, in a very attractive English work, *The Policy of the Metropolis.*[29] Among other things, it talked about how the Jewish community, limited solely to commerce, also makes itself guilty of so many transgressions, including interest, importing of counterfeit coins, and traffic in stolen goods. And there the author turns to its teachers, presiding officers, and elders, with the following reproach: "It is also much to be desired that the heads and leading persons of the Jewish religion would make it their duty to think of means to occupy their people with useful products and works, especially also the youth, who are currently growing up in idleness and dissoluteness. *If the strict, superstitious observance of legal regulations, such as what is required on the Sabbath and what is necessary for cattle to be slaughtered by Jews* (he could have spoken generally about the difference between clean and unclean foods) *exclude them now from useful businesses and from intermingling with the entire mass of people, so that they are not able to serve as messengers and become apprentices,* thus at least care should still be taken that they would not damage the state—an evil that necessarily must follow as long as they insist on their system, which is precisely a hindrance to the interests of the state and of morality."

Now that is, indeed, only one voice. The question would still be what the Parliament would decide if several Jews, following that same voice, presented themselves in London for citizenship; and also what the Lord Bishops in the Upper House in particular would have to say, who are otherwise so silent in the most important human affairs, such as the emancipation of slaves. Yet I have only excerpted this here in order to elucidate, with the view of a foreign author, what for me is, as I hope, a very proper judgment: through the renunciation of the ceremonial laws a great difficulty to you and your fellow brethren's naturalization would already be laid to rest; and in order to communicate to you his same philanthropic wish, that men of prominence among your people might at the outset make the meaning of renunciation more acceptable to him. For after a writing so masterful in every respect, it cannot be doubted that you, even if you are not voters among the same people, would have the prestige for that purpose.

29. [Eds.] We are unable to identify this pre-1799 title.

To this extent, I have thus placed myself with you, worthy esteemed friends, in the situation in which our Lord Christ found himself when one of the Jewish lawyers wanted to know from him: Which is the greatest commandment of them all? Indeed, he gave him this answer: *Love God fervently and your neighbor as yourself.* This lawyer affirmed in his reply that his answer was briefly and forcefully expressed, and even added for himself: "That is more than burnt offerings[30] and all sacrifices." According to the report of the historian,[31] Christ, having perceived that he thought *sensibly*, sent him away with the honorable reply, "You are not far from the kingdom of God," i.e., you have the proper understanding of the moral convictions solely pleasing to God, which even now I am to make valid among you; and it is thus now only a matter of you also complying with it in your conduct. In the same vein, he warned, on a similar occasion: "Do that, then you will live."[32] Thus, I say, Christ dismissed the man—Christ, who, according to his own declaration, *did not seek his own honor* and in consciousness of highest approval found his happiness and his contentment.[33] He did not require, just as on the occasion already sketched earlier, that the man consider himself bound to him and, as it were, should take his side; Christ trusted and hoped that the man would already make this good idea universal among his friends and acquaintances.

As you see, I am just not a maker of proselytes, for whom it is merely a matter of strengthening his party; in accordance with my principles, I really am not suited for that. Nonetheless, I give you my hand and my voice most willingly, as a member and even as a teacher of the Protestant church—indeed, only as one among many—if you join the same church and wish to confess to the Christianity purified from the time of the Reformation onward. To be sure, at the start it seemed to me to contradict that somewhat when you—and that with special emphasis in the printing—say

30. [Eds.] reading *Brandopfer* for *Braudopfer*.
31. Mark 12:29–34.
32. Luke 10:28.
33. John 8:50–4.

(page 68): "To abandon the religion of our fathers, i.e., the ceremonial laws, and to accept the Christian religion" would be for you *"entirely different* matters."

Yet, I thought, how are they so completely different? Did not all instructions, admonitions, and reproaches that our Lord Christ often made to the Jews have the effect of presenting those laws as no longer necessary and uniting the Jew and the Samaritan in one worship of God?

It was formerly often debated among Christian theologians whether Christ had only wanted to reform or to abrogate Judaism. I believe one could have been spared the entire controversy. What even you[34] say about the Mosaic practices falling away of their own accord under certain circumstances—that hence Moses did not need to explain himself expressly—is also valid here. The improvement and the abolition clearly flowed into one another. If he wanted the former, then he would also have to want the latter; and if the former occurred, the latter would follow by itself. For it was exactly the aforementioned law that made the great wall of division between Jews and other people of that time. Yet that this wall should be taken away with time, he even expressly assured in the pithy expression of John[35] that you have made your own,[36] "the time is coming when the true worshipers will worship the Father in spirit and in truth (through thoughts and deeds) in every place."

Further, how could his apostle Paul explain himself more strongly against all Jewish practices than when he says: "In Jesus Christ neither circumcision nor foreskin count as something, but rather *faith that is active in love; a new creature,*" a man of purified convictions; and when he generally—with the same sort of zeal for virtue—characterized every national difference as insignificant or unimportant on the scales of Christianity: *Here is neither Jew, nor Greek—You are always all one in Christ.*[37] Or when he

34. [Eds.] *OL,* 53: "If their [the ceremonies'] suitability as a means to this purpose ceased to apply, they had to be dispensed with or to be changed according to circumstances." *KGA* I.2, 391:24–8.

35. John 4:2.

36. [Eds.] *OL,* 77: "Would it not be more advisable to walk upon the slow path and to wait for time to unite all those who *serve God in spirit and truth?*" *KGA* I.2, 411, 37–8.

37. Galatians 3:28; 5:6; 6:15.

affirms, in the Letter to the Romans and in several chapters to the Galatians, that no man will become righteous through the works of Mosaic law.[38]

Yet I have understood you. You make a distinction, very proper in itself, between *truths of reason* and *truths of history*, of which the former truths permit conviction—a matter of the intellect—and the latter require faith, accordingly more a matter of the heart and of feeling, so that one is also accustomed to calling the latter *truths of faith*. You distinguish, ever so rightly, that *essential aspect* of religion from nonessential additions and how it underlies every truth that really is such; thus also do you distinguish Christianity. Or you contrast the *basis* of religion, as you also refer to it several times, with that which rests upon it—certain further principles. In other words, you distinguish fundamental from secondary teachings, religious principles from doctrines or dogmas. You even assert further—and this is generally admitted—that there is yet a middle category between *positive* religion and *irreligion*—the wholly pure, and, as one might characterize it, plain religion. These are, as I said, the properly considered uncontested decisions you touch upon several times in your *Open Letter*, such as pages 46–9 and 70–1, and have especially recorded on page 50[39] According to these distinctions, you now give assurance of wanting to be Christians—but only no middle thing between Jews and Christians—and thereby not wanting to found a special sect either in Judaism or in Christianity. You want to profess the truths of reason in Christianity, the essentials, the basic teachings, the actual religious principles of the same, yet not dogmas and what is nonessential or positive. You also desire to undertake baptism upon yourselves in the same prescribed manner and so enter the Protestant church, because you say this teaches the Christian religion more purely than other parties do and its spirit is milder and more tolerant. Finally, I should propose a Christian confession to you after these explanations and according to my judgment, which even I, placing myself in your situation, would be inclined to make from the heart, without reservations in thoughts and without playing with words. You

38. Romans 3:28.

39. [Eds.] In *OL*, Friedländer affirms the basic tenets of deism: God, immortality, human perfectibility, and happiness.

would not like to see the term <u>*Son of God*</u> used in your confession, on the grounds that it is ambiguous in the sacred documents of the New and Old Testament and thus without a more definite expression whereby you could deceive yourselves or others. Just as this now also honors your refined feeling of conscience, so indeed this entire challenge is no easy task for me. Although I am certainly no Moses, who, as had been noted earlier, resolved another sort of task happily, so I am certainly not lacking true religious seriousness to respond to you to the best of my ability.

To go in reverse order: what I at the end called the completely plain, undisguised religion is probably imaginable in intuition, removed from all sensory interference and will, of course, be thinkable for you. However, neither you nor another—even if still so much wiser and deeper-thinking—will in its selection be able to hold fast to it forever. This kind of religion can only occur in greater minds, and it even seems salutary for human beings never to possess it completely in pure form, if only the added ingredient is not too much and does not ruin its enjoyment entirely. In such a case it is like a dish that completely ruins one's health because of the many ingredients. This I postulate, so to speak, without proof and illustration, which the narrow boundaries I must set for my answer would not permit anyway.

Consequently, I only wanted to say that even you will have already had to accept something positive in and with the Christian religion. Indeed, you really also do that by finding the custom of *baptism* permissible for yourselves. And why should you not, since it is such a meaningful sign of the baptized person's commitment to the purity of heart and life; it should be, according to Christ's intention, and is therefore also recognized by the Protestant church for that purpose. It is exactly the same with the memorial celebration of Christ at communion, especially where, as in Brandenburg, no one is compelled any longer to turn up beforehand at the so-called confessional. Communion is not only an acknowledgment of Christ's glorious benefits rendered to humanity but also a kind of food for the soul through which all good convictions toward God and mankind and all resolutions for virtue are nourished or strengthened. Thereby, it does not matter at all what one consumes, but how one consumes it. This is a matter about which those in the Protestant church, or at least those among its teachers, are now also pretty much in agreement.

On the whole, I like to think of such simple, bloodless, uncom-
plicated ceremonies, which are possible for everyone to observe
(of which the ceremonies of your church were the opposite), as a
vehicle for the enjoyment of religion. With a sense of well-being
one is thereby more vividly aware than usual of religion's influence in strengthening a person for all good deeds and in comforting one for everything and in every way.[40] In addition, many a
man living in constant sensual desire is nevertheless forced at this
opportunity to reflect a little about himself and his higher calling.

Moreover, I also cannot in this way release you entirely from
believing. In that case I would have not understood you rightly,
and your opinion would have been solely aimed at the doctrine
of this or that worshiping society, which you mention once on
page 75.[41] I do not mean it this way! For we are all taught each
rational truth from childhood on by taking the truth of things on
authority; only afterwards do we, as it were, shake these off and
convince ourselves of them for our own reasons. To be exact, that
would not affect you, since you have already gained this personal
persuasion through practice in reflection and investigation. You
yourself even admit on page 71.[42] that historical truths can be
unusual, without this suspending their credibility, and so forth.
Indeed, you grant on pages 49, 50, and 51 that the external reasons of a rational truth can strengthen the internal ones or facilitate their persuasion for a majority of people.

Rather, I wanted to say that difference—conceded as such,
between rational and historical truths, between convictions and

40. Let it be said here only in passing that, already for this reason, I cannot
completely share your opinion, uttered on pages 61–2 [*KGA* I.2: 398, 9–25],
according to which the quantity of ceremonies are supposed to be less detrimental to morality than metaphysical dogmas are. Rather the more unimportant the
former and the more their meaning disappears in holy obscurity, all the more
thoughtlessly one observes them. And because one senses them, after all, as an
annoyance, the more one tends to blame the deity for the deficiency of one's own
one moral behavior. The aforesaid dogmas, on the contrary, surely sharpen the
intelligence, awaken the sense of conscience, and enliven it through the true,
which forms its basis.

41. [Eds.] Teller's point would appear to be that Friedländer in this passage
dodges the question of belief by acting as if the meaning of "Son of God" can only
be held as dogma.

42. [Eds.] *OL*, "It is the case that truths of history can be *unusual*; this does not
by itself destroy their credibility."

faith—does not always have to be taken so absolutely. It is correct to separate them in theory; but in practice they often merge, and reason, as it were, takes history as its support. The highest truth of the being of an omniscient creator of all things: on what is this based, if not on history—the history of that which happens day after day, in all of nature, according to eternal laws; the history of all changes that happen invariably in human society? So if you, dear friends, want to become Christians, then that which I therefore also expect from you, even if you do not expressly say it right away, will have to be first: that you accept Christ as the *founder of the better moral religion*. And in this way you at least proceed with this historical truth first based on faith, before that belief can turn into a conviction.

Now, in return for that I leave completely up to your *circumspect choice* the *doctrines,* which even Christianity has at one time or another more or less distorted, in contrast to the *fundamental teachings*. In order to embrace the latter, I at least do not like to bind any Christian soul to the former; I would be afraid of laying upon that person only another kind of yoke than the one from which Christ released us, his followers. For what are the *fundamental teachings* of Christianity? I consider them to be those without which Christians could not at all assert its cherished name. These are the ones that directly and immediately set the will in motion and that are capable of giving rise to views about God and mankind similar to Christ's; the calm mind must recognize them as true, and a not completely degenerate heart must grow fond of them. They are easy to grasp, easy to remember, and easy to put into practice without much expenditure of time and money. They are the *wisdom of life* that gently leads toward life's end, in the hope of a better one.

What, compared with that, are *doctrines?* I think they are—as our most respected theologians of former and recent times have always distinguished dogmas from fundamental teachings, and have done so in the same manner—the doctrines are, I say, what mere worship services are to religion—its expression as philosophy.[43] Since even doctrines, after all, have in view something

43. [Eds.] Doctrines, for Teller, like philosophy and worship, are secondary to fundamental religious teaching, which, for Enlightenment theology, arises from the morality of Christ.

beneficial, they may be a quite useful occupation of the mind, an exercise of intelligence for those who have time to spare or who feel an inner calling. They may, then, also be, for each person, what they can be, as long as one does not impose them in a domineering way on others who develop no taste for them. For doctrines are also more like a dry *science* that chills the heart, causes quarrels and feuds and, frequently, the far-flung separation of those who nevertheless, according to a strange contradiction, pray to One God and Father. Yet when the end comes, this dry science has to make room for that peaceable and friendly wisdom in the mind of the one who is dying, so that only trust in God, trust in His forgiving mercy and rewarding love, remains one's final support. And may nevertheless all the disturbers of the peace in Christianity, especially we theologians—as valiant comrades-in-arms of their Lord against crude disbelief, gloomy superstition, and the prevailing depravity—make Christ's invitation their daily battle cry: *Come unto me—take my yoke upon you, and learn from me,* all of you who are subjugated by your priests and think you will succumb under the burden of worship ceremonies! *For my yoke is easy and my burden is light.*[44] This invitation is surely just as gentle as the idea itself. However, what a hard yoke and what a heavy burden it is when even now too much scholarly knowledge is forced upon youth, as well as upon entire congregations, in the instruction of religion. To be sure, one cannot fail to recognize the discernment with which even the essentials of Christianity are blended with the externalities and, if I may use this phrase, are kneaded together. However, those well versed in language and history also know through what causes that has occurred from century to century since the Apostolic age. And so at least no popular teacher should pay further attention to that but should understand how to separate the dissimilar parts from the pure substance.

So, then, venerable men, I do not wish to lay upon you a yoke of a different kind, as I have already commented. Rather, with the impartiality to which your trust also especially obligates me I simply point you back to that basic teaching of Christianity, to the truth *that Christ is the founder, chosen and sent by God, of a better religion than your entire previous ceremonial practice was and could be; that*

44. Matthew 11:29–30.

Christ is the Lord, the head of all who choose him for themselves as the forerunner in the true worship of God and who follow his instructions—in short, the head of the congregation, as Paul in particular portrayed him in this light in his letter to the Ephesians.[45] And with that you have also embraced the true, practical Christianity, as in one kernel. For example, you have the fundamental teachings: that God is the Father of all people, without national distinctions; that he wants to be worshiped in spirit and in truth, which means through every kind of upright conduct; that you owe thanks, love, and honor to Christ himself, the great friend of humanity and herald of a new covenant with God, which your prophets[46] caught a glimpse of only in the far distance; and that you are obligated to become like him in his holy purpose. You really cannot know, after all, which and how many sparks from the light of his teachings that have bathed you so long in Christianity have alighted in your souls. You cannot know which, be it many or few, have contributed to the fact that you were able to imprint upon your open letter so many correct insights and so much love of virtue, certainly with the approval of all readers, even if they still think in the main so disparagingly of you.

Therefore you will also not take it amiss when I claim that in Christianity the recognition of what you call the *eternal truths* existed earlier in their purity and has all along spread more generally among the Christians than among your fellow believers. And thus also, if I may use this simile, the bright light of the eternal truths that has illuminated the way for us has at the same time shed more light upon the bypath along which you have gone! To use another comparison: the purer, gentler air of the Gospels has also breathed upon you. And actually, who, besides Christ, had really and truly made it his business to spread practical religion among the people, to popularize it? Not one of the ancient philosophers. They carried on their business for themselves and left the people to their own devices. Even Socrates had only his selection of pupils.

Now, however, while I would make only what I have previously noted the main issue for you, upon admission to the Protestant church, as pupils eager to learn (as I take you to be for the

45. Ephesians 1:22–3; 4:15; 5:23.
46. Jeremiah 31:31–4.

time being, without, however, wanting to give myself the standing of your teacher), I thus consider myself to be acting in the spirit of Christ and his chosen messengers.

Whom did Christ himself admit into his society? What did he require of them? Namely, that they recognize the one true God, who is not only the God of the Jews but of all peoples, and that they recognize Christ as his ambassador, who through his entire enterprise glorified (i.e., illumined) the Father, made His will known to them, and reassured them, under this condition: of God's love. Since they received those words, they were thus his dear disciples, to whom he at the end bore such laudable witness.[47] This happened regardless of the fact that they were still lacking much in the way of proper knowledge, as was the case with Peter, who did not understand that the non-Jewish peoples should also take part in the new religious society. Christ promoted the belief that he is a *light of the world*, a teacher of people.[48] He was satisfied as soon as Peter accepted him as the *Christ* (the anointed one) of God. This same Peter himself required only the belief that God had made Jesus *Lord* and *Christ*,[49] just as John did at the end of his account. And when Paul wanted to declare the basic teachings of the religion of the new covenant, he described them with these few words: *Jesus Christ*—Christ is the ambassador of God; Jesus, who came into the world to become a helper, a savior of humanity—which was lost in superstition, or disbelief, or wickedness. And Paul left it up to each individual's conscience what he, as teacher, intended to build upon that basic teaching, whether a massive building, or simply one of wood, clay, or straw.[50] Furthermore, when he wanted to describe the high majesty that each person ought to recognize in the person of Christ, he explained it this way: God has given him *a name*, a majesty, an authority *that is above all names*, which surpasses all human titles; *that in his name*, on the basis of his authority, *all who are in heaven and on earth and under the earth*, the learned and the untaught—yes, even those still completely unaware—shall bend their knees *to the honor of God the Father*, and *all tongues* shall confess that *Jesus*

47. John 17:3, 4, 6, 8.
48. John 8:12; 12:46. Cf. 12:35–6 and 1:4–9.
49. Luke 9:21; Acts 2:36.
50. 1 Corinthians 3:11–2.

Christ is the Lord.[51] You, however, esteemed friends, know better than anyone that, even according to the language of the Talmud, which was in existence already in Paul's time, even though not in one compilation, *people of the earth,* yom ha'aretz, meant the rabble, or also, the laity; *people of heaven* meant the wise ones and the scholars, although I would not argue with anyone who wants to interpret these terms as high and low, or even the lowest. Now just as Paul wrote in this way to his Philippians to profess Christ as Lord, Master, and Teacher, so he also taught other congregations accordingly: "We *preach* Christ, that *he is the Lord.*"[52]

If you still want, however, a somewhat expanded *confession,* which contains in it all the aforesaid fundamental teachings and is purely apostolic, there is by no means a lack thereof. I do not thereby mean our so-called *Apostles' Creed,* which, to be sure, minus the historically proven additions that it gradually accrued, is not to be rejected, but which nevertheless was not composed by the apostles themselves. Rather, I understand the following, which Paul prescribed to the congregation at Ephesus,[53] for which I will only append the more correct German translation:

"*One body* and *one spirit,* one single community enlivened by one spirit; and thus one and *the same hope in God,* to which all are called; *One Lord,* head of the congregation (Christ); *one faith;* one religion; *one baptism; one God and Father of all, who is there above you all, and through all of you and in all of you,* the supreme Lord of all of you, through whom he carries out his counsel and in whom he brings about all good things."

Now after all that, the formula that one could use at your baptism, since precisely you are descended from Judaism, would be the following, from which one can assume, according to the clear report in Acts,[54] that *Peter* and *Paul* used it: "*I baptize you with the name* [Jesus Christ]," or as it actually should be translated, "*with the confession of Christ,*" and—what perhaps should still be added—[who is] the founder of a more spiritual and more gladdening religion than that which the community to which you

51. Philippians 2:9–11.

52. 2 Corinthians 4:5. Cf. the previously cited passages from the letter to the Ephesians.

53. Ephesians 4:4, 5, 6 of the letter to the aforementioned community.

54. Acts 2:38; 19:5.

have belonged until now professes. Thus it is probable that the formula in *Matthew* that we usually use, especially also in a context where it was a question of the conversion of non-Jewish nations—"go into all the world and teach all the nations,"[55]—was meant more for the pagans. Perhaps *Peter* received a special instruction from Christ for the use of the former confession in the baptism of the Jews.

Nonetheless, you would also find it harmless to have yourselves baptized according to the second one, even if yet another special, more precise provision were added, of God as the *Father of all people,* because this must also be a basic teaching for you who come forth from Judaism; *of Christ as humanity's savior from unbelief, as well as from superstition and all sins;* of the Holy Spirit as that *which shall have in us its work.*[56]

Now all of this is my private judgment, as you have requested. I do not know how many or how few among my fellow brethren, the teachers of the Protestant church, would want to concur with me in this. Similarly, it would have called for too extensive a consultation about it with the royal council, of which I have the honor of being a member, in order to obtain its opinion about the matter. However, on my own account I can believe them, especially the last-mentioned patrons and friends, who are very dear to me, capable of the basic idea which your Moses urged upon heads of households when he made the lenient treatment of their slaves a duty: "Remember that you, too, were slaves in Egypt."[57] Thus, I say, all Protestant teachers will also set a good example in this regard for their congregations. They, too, will remember that for a long time their forefathers were slaves under a tyrannical yoke, until the time of the Reformation; they struggled for a long

55. [Eds.] Matthew 28:19.

56. [Eds.] A partial allusion to Paul's "gifts of the spirit" passage, 1 Corinthians 12:4–7: "Now there are diversities of gifts, but the same Spirit. And there are differences of administrations, but the same Lord. And there are diversities of operations, but it is the same God which worketh all in all. But the manifestation of the Spirit is given to every man to profit withal."

57. Deuteronomy 24:15.

time until they were liberated from it and were able to gain the Protestant freedom. They will not fail to apply also to you[58] the spirit of tolerance, which not only has become ever more prevalent among themselves, but which they have also shown toward a *third* party which has arisen among them since the middle of this century, a denomination called the *Moravian Brethren*.[59] Finally, they will think like the wise, tolerant, and pious Gamaliel, about whom one does not even need to know anything more in order to acknowledge him for this: *"If it is a work of human beings, then it will founder; if it is from God, then you cannot suppress it."*[60]

Just as my whole appraisal is only that, and only the judgment of a Protestant teacher, thus this is also a question completely independent of it: what and how much of the civil rights and liberties might a Christian state find advisable—for it itself and in accordance with its constitution—to grant to you on the basis of such a confession? The reply to this question belongs in a completely different forum, according to the relationship in which state and church stand vis-à-vis each other.

Namely, this relationship can be thought of in three ways. *Either* the state and church are one and the same and flow, so to speak, completely into each other; *or* they are united; *or* the church is by itself in the state and subject only to the latter's general supervision, like every other association which convenes for a useful purpose and is known for that.

The first, as you yourself have observed on page 53, was the case with your theocracy.[61] The deity was the head of the country as well as the church, as it were, in one person; all institutions of worship were at the same time civil ones, and vice versa. It was one and the same constitution. Thus it was a matter of course that no non-Israelite ecclesiastical community could occupy a place

58. [Eds.]: Reading *Sie* for *sie*.

59. One cannot even actually say in this sense "party," since even they count themselves among the evangelicals according to the imperial peace treaty [1648 Peace of Westphalia], and thus among the Protestants. They have therefore been granted civil rights and liberties in imperial electoral matters, even if they themselves admit right away they avail themselves of different methods, which they call *tropi*, in order to accommodate the weak.

60. Acts 5:38–9.

61. [Eds.] *OL*, "State and religion were not separate, but one; not connected, but still the same."

therein, and so also none of such a community's members could attain citizenship. All that was conceded to the foreigner who did not completely convert to the congregation and only committed himself to observance of the seven Noachide commandments was that he was permitted, in the Hebraic manner of speaking, *to enter and exit the gates* and to settle as an inhabitant.

It has been the second case in Christian states since Christianity was no longer merely tolerated but had become the state religion under Constantine the Great. Then state and church and church and state were joined together and have, for the most part, remained so in Christianity since that time. Nonetheless, this union has existed in such a way, so to speak, that the ranking order has alternated. Under Constantine until Theodosius the Great it was called *state and church*, and the latter was subordinate to the former. Subsequently, and with the increasing prestige of the Roman bishop, the situation changed: the church seized the upper hand, so that one now said *church and state*, until the Reformation restored the previous ranking order. The provincial sovereigns had done the church a great service: at least looking after the theologians, also probably protecting them on the quiet, as especially the prince elector in Saxony did, promoting the great change.[62] Religious peace came about.

It had not been possible to break away from the immense concept of a *universal* Christian church extending over the whole world, in agreement with all main and subordinate points, which assumed there must necessarily be one visible head who keeps everything in order.[63] So in each province that had accepted the Reformation a regent was simultaneously appointed as head of the Protestant church that had come into being there. He was entrusted with all rights that the bishop of Rome had maintained

62. [Eds.] An allusion to Frederick the Wise (1463–1525), Prince Elector of Saxony who consistently championed Luther against the papacy and became the protector of the Protestant reformer, thus ensuring the initial success of the Reformation.

63. [Eds.] The passage alludes to the Peace of Augsburg (September 25, 1555), which treated the confessional disruption of Catholic and Protestant through a partial political solution in which the two religious confessions in Germany achieved a state of coexistence: the religion of the head of each state determined the legal religion of his subjects around the slogan *cuius regio, eius religion,* or "whose region, his religion."

over the Catholic church. Now, to be sure, the order had been restored by which the church was subordinated to the state, as in earlier times. However, there was something illogical about the fact that the reformers, who had also wanted to destroy all papal prestige, now nevertheless gave it to every provincial sovereign. Thus each Protestant province had its pope. It therefore came about that so-called religious courts, called *consistories*, were founded. They decided all marital matters as well as offences of pastors and schoolteachers and their dismissal or removal. Subsequently, a Carpzov[64] in Saxony organized this so-called *protestant church law* into an orderly system. This prevailed until Justus Henning Böhmer[65] in Halle later showed, in his larger work on this church law, the following: that what Carpzov and his successors had derived from the transfer of rights in church affairs from the archbishop to the provincial sovereign was already, in large part, due the sovereign as the possessor of the superior power in the state.

Böhmer, as noted, approached the *third* kind of relationship, which can be thought of as the state versus the church and the church versus the state. I have treated this type at greater length than both of the other, less difficult ones in a separate treatise.[66] Here I will only summarize it briefly. In that case every Christian church—whose founder already himself declared: "*My kingdom, the kingdom of truth and virtue, is not of this world*—it does not interfere with any earthly government, it does not quarrel with any. Rather, it favors the one like the other"[67]—is to be considered

---

64. [Eds.] Benedikt Carpzov (1595–1666), a professor in Leipzig, created a complete system of Protestant church law, *Jurisprudentia ecclesiastica*, in 1645.

65. [Eds.] Justus Henning Böhmer, (1674–1749), a professor in Halle after 1701, represented a moderate form of Enlightenment "territorialism," which places the church under state law. His works include the six-volume *Ius ecclesiasticum Protestantium* (Halle: Waisenhaus, 1714–36, 1756–89, 5th Edition).

66. *Valentinian the First, or Conversations of a Monarch with His Successor to the Throne about the Religious Freedom of Subjects, 2nd edition.* [Wilhelm Abraham Teller, *Valentinian der Erste oder geheime Unterredungen eines Monarchen mit seinem Thronfolger über die Religionsfreiheit der Unterthanen* (Berlin: Mylius, 2. Auflage, 1791).]

67. [Eds.] Adapted from John 18:36: "Jesus answered, My kingdom is not of this world: if my kingdom were of this world, then would my servants fight, that I should not be delivered to the Jews: but now is my kingdom not from hence." (King James Version)

in every kingdom and land like every association that has a good
purpose and convenes at certain times and on certain designated
premises in order to further its common good. In an ecclesiastical
society, this common good is the most edifying communal worship of God possible and the mutual awakening to do so, according to the religious principles to which all members agree. The
sovereign of the province thus only takes this ecclesiastical society under his supervision—assures himself about what takes
place in it, what its principles are, who are its directors, on whom
he can rely in any given case. If he does not have any misgivings
on behalf of the state, then he protects its members as good citizens. If disputes arise within the ecclesiastical society, or with its
teachers, then he has the proper court administer justice and
make a judicial pronouncement that accords with its contracts
related to the matter.

Each church, then, also has its own consistory or presbytery,
which, as in the first Christian church, consists of *elders* and dea-
cons, who, however, have no binding power whatsoever. There
can, in a city, be several such congregations that, although of the
same confession, nevertheless have no more precise connection
than that among themselves. Accordingly, each member must be
at liberty to leave one and join another neighboring one. In the
same way, no one must be forced to join a particular congregation; it does not put a civil blemish upon someone who does not
join any. Here, then, is complete Christian liberty in a major affair
of the conscience, which also, as stated, can never, under the
oversight of the state, be misused as the pretext for malice and
secret intrigues. And here not religion but the civil bond unites
state and church. The church does not run alongside the state as a
secondary power, but rather religion is in the state as a subordinate that, like every vassal and every local authority, owes the
state its duties for the state's protection. Religion, however, will
perform them all the more willingly the more the state treats religion's conscience with care.

As I stated, Böhmer came close to this third external constitution of the Christian church. Therefore, for a long time after him
only disciplinary matters were left up to the consistories in Prussian provinces. All truly legal matters, however, in divorces and
such, were assigned to the civil courts. And it was also precisely
this very constitution that the National Assembly in France agreed

to, according to its first constitution, as I had it reprinted in my *Magazine for Preachers*.[68] However, it was unfortunately destroyed with the royal office of kingship. And now the *united North American states* are the only ones, at least eleven among the sixteen states that of late belong to them, in which this constitution is in force. These include *Rhode Island, New York, Pennsylvania, Virginia, North Carolina, Georgia, and so forth.* The government allows all ecclesiastical societies the free exercise of their worship services so long as they are not detrimental to or dangerous for the civil peace and security. The government does not contribute anything to the construction of church buildings or the salary of teachers, but it also does not hamper the ecclesiastical societies as regards either. The government obligates citizens only either to the *belief in God* and to obedience of the laws, or to the *Christian* religion generally, without a closer determination of a particular denomination, and to the assumed obedience. I have likewise provided documents about this matter in the sixth volume, first article of the *Magazine*.

Now, as I have already observed, that is not, however, the fundamental constitution in the European Protestant countries. The so-called state interest or even the real welfare of the state can often intervene in a religious confession which, as such, the government could indeed well recognize as Protestant, but in a way that the government can have reservations about granting civil liberties and the advantages thereof. An example is the following case: The Protestants divide into two main denominations, those pure and simply so-called *Evangelicals*, (since they also, like the Silesians, would do well in not labeling themselves with the sectarian apposition *Lutheran*), and the *Evangelical Reformed*, or simply *Reformed*. They called themselves *Protestants* because the reformers, their ancestors, had solemnly protested against a very insidious mandate of Emperor Charles V "to let rest the quarrels with the Roman Catholics until a general church assembly and in the meantime leave everything in its old state," an edict therefore called the *Interim*.[69] And it is certainly thanks to the Brandenburg

---

68. *Magazin für Prediger*, second article in volume 4. [Teller edited the *Neues Magazin für Prediger* (Jena/Leipzig: Fromann), which ran from volume 1 in 1792–3 to volume 10 in 1801–2.

69. [Eds.] The Augsburg Interim, promulgated June 30, 1548, sought to regulate Protestant and Catholic confessions upon order of the political authorities.

theologians that these two denominations revived this designation [Protestant] and jointly gave it to themselves in order to testify to their mutual unity of mind, despite many a difference of opinion, as those who protest against all intolerance toward those who confess a different religion. At least this is how I would construe the term.

Now let us imagine a land in which only one of these two denominations has public freedom of religion with all civil advantages, whose regent is, however, Roman Catholic and therefore must, upon taking up his governmental office, solemnly promise to let the previous constitution stand as is in regard to the religion of his subjects. If one further supposes that the more-favored Protestant faction wanted to grant the less-favored faction more liberties, what does the former have to fear? I think that either the regent, if he is a just man, will not and must not allow this closer coming together of both Protestant factions—he will and must hinder it himself, because the oath he gave obligates him to do so—or, if he is not a just man and is silent about the matter, he will shortly call for more rights for his own fellow believers.[70]

Here, then, very esteemed friends, where your conversion to the Protestant church at the same time becomes a matter of the state, it is proper for me to put down my pen. However, I cannot do it without taking leave from you, in imitation of Christ, with the wish and hope that your great, important matter induces in me. You say on page 48, "What we have chosen may still need many a correction and may be amenable to many additions," and so forth. Even that, too, is meant and stated just as modestly as it reveals a heart that is opened to every truth yet to be recognized—that sensitive, good heart which our Lord Christ praised so highly.[71] Thus you will, then, preserve this heart for everything that, for instance, your insights and convictions might still lack in regard to the content of the Christian religion. You will penetrate more deeply into the spirit of Christianity and always be mindful of Christ's utterance on the title page of this response. Paul also alludes to it when he says, "The letter (of your ceremonial law)

---

70. [Eds.] By showing the independence of state authority and obligations vis-à-vis religion, Teller also indicates the rightful place of this authority in deciding the merits of David Friedländer's case for Jewish citizenship.

71. Luke 3:15.

kills, suppresses, frightens with everlasting fear of punishment and death, but the *spirit* (the Gospel) gives *life,* rouses one to everything good and pleasing.[72] Even you concede on page 45 that the ceremonial law kills.[73] And so may then the *spirit of truth* continue, as until now, to rest upon you, the spirit which *was to lead* the first disciples of Christ *into all truth* after his separation from them, although they had already been accepted by him and were loved by him.[74]

POSTSCRIPT
to all especially expert readers of this response.

The open letter made a sensation and has already called forth a number of dissimilar judgments and will also be assessed in publications of various kinds. This difference of opinions, as it cannot be assumed otherwise among people of diverse manner of thought and mind, is always a gain for truth, as long as stormy passions do not interfere with it. Excluding that, however intensely opinion may chafe on opinion, many a spark of truth will leap forth. In such a way will the voices about the preceding response, quite naturally, also be divided. One faction will think I should not have answered at all; another and, as I presume, a larger one will think the answer should and could have been done in another fashion, be it this or that.

Since I gladly credit both factions with proceeding in this matter upon principles that simply are not mine, it would be arrogant of me if I wanted to dispute the right of either to an independent judgment. I only felt I owed to the trust put in me, and to the matter itself, some kind of humane response. I therefore also promised to answer publicly, in order to leave no room open for regret. May the judgment itself, however, turn out as it will, whether its outcome be this or that; thus I will welcome

72. 2 Corinthians 3:6.

73. [Eds.] *OL:* "The positive laws are embarrassing, burdened with costs, and wasteful of time; the negative ones set up barriers to his [a young Jewish man's] activity in our common life."

74. John 16:13.

reading a great many opinions about my answer, no matter how far divergent from mine, and quietly make the best possible use of them for myself. *Let us therefore,* even in this matter, *follow after the things that make for peace, and things wherewith one may edify another!* (Romans 14:19)[75]

---

75. A correction: Just after finishing the second edition, I was made aware of a lapse of memory. On page 141 [of the present text], which concerns the *Interim*—it was not pushed through by Charles V in 1548 as a compromise attempt between the Roman Catholics and the Protestants, since the intended mandate was already granted in 1529. Thus the words "therefore called the *Interim*" are omitted.

A Postscript:
Contemporary Parallels
and Permutations

One could, after all, quite unbureaucratically grant citizenship to a million people overnight. That is no problem. . . . The people are registered; it is a completely organized country. One can solve it quite simply. But somehow the politicians are afraid of this, and I don't understand this fear, because they don't get rid of the people by this method, either. In this way, foreigners—so to-speak eternal foreigners in Germany—will be produced by themselves for further generations.[1]

The Turkish-German Case

Except for the numbers cited, one might suspect these sentiments belonged to one of the documents translated from the 1799 debate; it is reminiscent of the sardonic speculations of the anonymous author of the "Political-Theological Task" about the wisdom of mass baptism as the cure for the alleged foibles of the Jews and the gateway to all civil rights and freedoms (34). But taken as a serious suggestion, it is closer to Schleiermacher's rejection of religion-based criteria for citizenship, when he argues that reason "demands that all should be citizens, but it does not require that all must be Christians" (85). Indeed, the passage

1. "*Man könnte ja auch ganz unbürokratisch einer Million Leute die Staatsbürgerschaft über Nacht geben. Das ist kein Problem. . . . die Leute sind registriert, es ist ein voll organisiertes Land. . . . Ganz einfach kann man das losen. Aber irgendwie hat die Politik anscheinend Angst davor und ich verstehe diese Angst nicht. . . . Denn so werden sie die Leute auch nicht los. So werden dann Fremde, sozusagen ewige Fremde in Deutschland für weitere Generationen selbst produziert.*" Zafer Şenocak, interview with Dursun Tan, 1996, quoted by Hans-Peter Waldhoff, "Ein Übersetzer. Über die soziobiographische Genese eines transnationalen Denkstils,"*Brücken zwischen Zivilisationen: zur Zivilisierung ethnisch-kultureller Differenzen und Machtungleichheiten : das türkisch-deutsche Beispiel*, ed. Hans-Peter Waldhoff, Dursun Tan, and Elçin Kürsat-Ahlers (Frankfurt am Main:Verlag für Interkulturelle Kommunikation, 1997), 354. Unless otherwise noted, all translations from German are mine.

145

identifies the same sort of perspicacity essential for sorting out the factors hindering true integration of minorities in a society.

Moreover, the stated consequences of inaction, namely, the creation of the eternal foreigner, recall Schleiermacher's sensitivity to the self-perpetuating circle—whether of Jewish or German creation—which he saw as effectively hindering Jewish civil integration: the emphasis on Jews as an entity (a "nation") with ultimate loyalties to a purported fatherland beyond the state only undermines the formation of civil loyalties and protracts their status as interim residents not eligible for citizenship, thereby making them eternal foreigners (*Fourth Letter*).[2]

Actually, the author of the above passage is Zafer Şenocak, a German-Turkish poet, political journalist, and social critic (1960–), addressing the question of German citizenship for Turkish residents in the Federal Republic of Germany. His words were quoted by the German sociologists Elçin Kürsat-Ahlers and Hans-Peter Waldhoff in their testimony before the German Bundestag debate to support the historic citizenship bill passed on May 7, 1999.[3] Effective January 1, 2000, the "Act to Amend the Nationality Law"(*Reform des Staatsangehörigkeitsrecht*) essentially transforms the acquisition of citizenship from a matter of "discretionary naturalization" to an act of political entitlement.[4] Its provisions not only shorten the time period before application for citizenship (from fifteen years to eight), but, above all, set conditions under which German-born children of foreign nationals have the option of choosing German citizenship at age

2. Schleiermacher points to Friedländer's contradictory views in lamenting the treatment of the Jews as foreigners but also speaking of them as a "nation." See also the introduction to this volume (1–29) and Schleiermacher's explanation (103–4).

3. Elçin Kürsat-Ahlers and Hans-Peter Waldhoff, "Auch die Einwanderer sind das Volk. Auszüge aus einer Stellungnahme zur Reform des Staatsangehörigkeitsrechts vor dem Bundestag," *Frankfurter Rundschau online*, May 7, 1999: 3–4 <www.fr-aktuell.de/fr/spezial/doppelpass.t723003.htm>.

4. Gerald L. Neuman, "Nationality Law in the United States and the Federal Republic of Germany: Structure and Current Problems," in *Paths to Inclusion: The Integration of Migrants in the United States and Germany*, ed. Peter H. Schuck and Rainer Münz (New York: Berghahn, 1998), 265 [quoted from Leslie Adelson, "Coordinates of Orientation: An Introduction," in Zafer Şenocak, *Atlas of a Tropical Germany: Essays on Politics and Culture, 1990–1998*, tr. and ed. Leslie A. Adelson (Lincoln, NE: University of Nebraska Press, 2000) xvii.]

twenty-three.[5] With the principle of place of birth (*ius soli*) thus augmenting the principle of blood lineage (*ius sanguinis*), German practices will begin to match more closely those of the other states of the European Union. Although this law's provisions do not go far enough for some critics (it has no provisions for generalized dual citizenship), the new legal status at least supports the possibility that public attitudes, represented for some by Martin Walser's reference to resident foreign nationals as "those billeted among us," will eventually reflect the reality of Germany as a multiethnic society.[6]

The Persistence of Ethnic Essentialism, 1799–1999

The relevancy of quoting Şenocak's remarks as late as 1999 underscores just how problematic the attitudes towards citizenship and community membership have continued to be over the more than two hundred years after the 1799 debate on Jewish emancipation. Indeed, it is hard to follow the debate about Jewish emancipation in Prussia without a profound sense of poignancy about the fate of European Jews in the intervening centuries. Why is it that none of the paths suggested by the contributors to the 1799 exchanges, whether made as provocation or in earnest,

5. The law stipulates that foreigners living legally in Germany may apply for citizenship after eight, instead of fifteen years, provided they 1) do not have a criminal record, 2) do not pursue anti-constitutional goals, 3) have a satisfactory command of the German language, and 4) give up their previous citizenship, unless qualified for an exception based on specified kinds hardship (including the status of political refugee). Any child still under ten years old on January 1, 2000, or born on that date or later, with at least one parent who has legally lived in the Federal Republic for eight years, must choose by age twenty-three either German citizenship or the citizenship of the parents. Failure to specify the option at that age will result in the loss of German citizenship, although in certain cases one may retain both citizenships. Children born of German citizens living outside Germany will lose their right to citizenship if the parents do not register them with the German government by the child's first birthday ("Einen Doppelpaß nur auf Zeit. Im Blickpunk: Staatsangehörigkeitsrecht," *Frankfurter Rundschau online*, May 7, 1999: 1, <http://www.fr-aktuell.de/fr/spezial/doppelpass/t732002.htm>.

6. Martin Walser's remarks appeared in article on national identity titled "Deutsche Sorgen," in *Der Spiegel* 47.26 (June 28, 1993): 45 (quoted in Şenocak, 95, 101 n.10).

resulted in a truly adequate basis for civil rights and protections that might have prevented the genocidal policies of the Third Reich? What are the factors that still make xenophobia, anti-Semitism, and racism so intractable, not only for the Federal Republic of Germany, but for any nation dealing today with migration and the challenges of fostering a truly multicultural society? It is crucial that modern societies seek answers to these questions if the vicious cycle is to be broken.

What Kürsat-Ahlers and Waldhoff have observed about the roots of current attitudes also adds to the understanding of the 1799 situation: the stronger the emphasis on ethnicity in defining the dominant political culture, the more the emphasis will be given to the ethnic identity of the non-citizens, especially if the ethnic majority's images of society and human beings are institutionalized in the law.[7] They identify this phenomenon as ethnic essentialism, which they define as the "silent assumption of the immutability of hereditary communities, [which becomes] the most radical when immutability is conceived as race."[8] For all the emphasis in the 1799 debate on reform and/or abandonment of Jewish religious ceremonies and a period of education for potential new citizens, the confounding issue facing the Jewish householders was ultimately this state-supported ethnic essentialism, with all its racist implications.

To be sure, Schleiermacher criticizes the Prussian state for its inactivity in the issue of Jewish emancipation (85–6). He rejects the practice of baptism as unworthy of both parties as a gateway to citizenship, at least in part because he, like the Jewish authors, finds offensive the underlying assumptions about the Jews' supposedly inherent moral corruption. However, Schleiermacher does not really question the underlying insistence on ethnic, i.e., biological, heredity as the unchanging basis of political self-definition for the

7. "Je stärker die politische Kultur eines Einwanderungslandes ethnisiert ist, desto stärker ethnisiert sie auch ihre Einwanderer. Die 'Ethnisierung des Rechts' bedeutet eine institutionelle Verfestigung entsprechender Gesellschaftsbilder und Menschenmodelle." Kürsat-Ahlers and Waldhoff, 2–3.

8. "[Es] zeigt sich, was wir 'substanzialistisch' and dieser politischen Kultur nennen, nämlich die stillschweigende Annahme der Unveränderlichkeit von Abstammungsgemeinschaften, am radikalsten, wenn diese Unveränderlichkeit biologisch als 'Rasse' gedacht wird" (Kürsat-Ahlers and Waldhoff, 2). I use "essentialism" here to translate their German term *substantialistisch*."

dominant German populace of the Prussian state; he does not fully address the allusion made by the author of the "Political-Theological Task" to the biological component, albeit somewhat buried in his satirical litany of possible reasons for denying civil rights to Jews.[9] Yet without this ethnic essentialism it is hard to understand Schleiermacher's argument for the persistence of one's birth religion, even if he notes Friedländer's concurrence, as the lone reason for insisting that a Jew will remain a Jew.[10] Indeed, his arguments reflect the repressed—or at least tacit—and still unresolved conflation of Jewish religion, culture, and biological lineage.

In fairness to Schleiermacher, a recurrent factor in the age-old search for German political unity has been the very lack of clarity in the distinctions between the state as a politically and legally defined territorial entity, and a nation "as an aggregate existing independent of state organization, unified by certain commonalities such as language, religion, culture, history, and descent."[11] As Kürsat-Ahlers and Waldhoff point out, the territorial fragmentation following the Thirty Years' War and the concomitant longing for German unity and restoration of empire it engendered help explain why the hereditary principle was viewed right into the 19th century as modern and overarching; hereditary affiliation that crossed borders undercut the old territorial principle that attached inhabitants to a feudal ruler. But it also created the phenomenon of the foreigner, with the concomitant intolerance of the outsider.[12] Although the political entity "Germany" that was created in 1871 did not encompass all Germans (notably, Austrians were not included) it was nevertheless understood as the fulfillment of the dream of nationhood, as the reification of ethnic German cohesiveness. Its citizenship law was thus a remnant of the North German Alliance, which was based on integration of the German tribes.[13]

9. "Rather it must be sought more deeply in their character, their convictions, their education, in a certain ill-humor, perversion, uselessness of their physical and mental capabilities, on account of which they are totally unreceptive to the enjoyment of those civil blessings. One must assume that through an inherited mixture of bodily fluids their physical powers have been weakened or numbed. . . ." (33)

10. See *Third Letter*, 100.

11. Neuman, 250 (quoted in Adelson, xviii).

12. Kürsat-Ahlers and Waldhoff, 3.

13. *Ibid.*

To be sure, the Imperial Citizenship Law (*Reichs- und Staats-angehörigkeitsgesetz*) of 1913 granted citizenship to Jews, but it nonetheless reaffirmed the essentialist principle of a hereditary community. Klaus J. Bade observes that this law was directed as much at safeguarding the continued citizenship of German transatlantic emigrants as at controlling immigration to Germany and as such was not unique to German thinking about transnational immigration affairs. Nonetheless, he also affirms the peculiarity and huge influence of the "ethno-national thinking" it reflected.[14]

By itself, then, the long-sought-for enfranchisement of the Jews could hardly effect attitudinal changes sufficiently to counteract the growing anti-Semitism that culminated in the policies of the Third Reich. Neither these legal provisions nor assimilation through baptism and/or intermarriage proved effective safeguards. Ironically, German church records of baptism, with their meticulous genealogical information, themselves became weapons against converted Jews and their progeny, when in 1935 the Nazis' anti-Jewish laws forced all Germans to disclose their ethnic lineage; such information aided the Nazis in their pernicious and relentless drive to ferret out, disenfranchise, harass, and, ultimately, to exterminate as many German and European Jews as possible. David Friedländer's words that "one no longer persecutes [the Jews] with fire and the sword" (61) stand in chilling contrast to the reality of Auschwitz.

Jewish Assimilation in the 20th Century: The Examples of Gerty Spies and Viktor Klemperer

It is equally poignant to realize how fervently many German Jews continued to pursue and believe in acculturation, despite mistreatment and persecution before and after Hitler's rise to power. Representative of countless others in her generation, German-Jewish novelist and concentration camp survivor Gerty

14. Klaus J. Bade, "Immigration, Naturalization, and Ethno-National Traditions in Germany: From the Citizenship Law of 1913 to the Law of 1999," in *Crossing Boundaries: The Exclusion and Inclusion of Minorities in Germany and Austria*, ed. Larry Eugene Jones (New York: Berghahn Books, 2001), 30. See also Gerald L. Neuman's previously noted article for a fuller treatment of the background factors and implications of this law.

Spies relates in *Drei Jahre Theresienstadt* the various instances of anti-Semitism she routinely experienced in her childhood, before and during World War I.[15] Reminiscent of Friedländer's description of society's use of the term "Jude" as a contemptuous epithet, Spies tells of a schoolmate who harassed her on the way home from school, yelling "Jud, Jud, Jud."[16] For this precocious Jewish girl child, these and other incidents, however unpleasant, were not yet perceived as life-threatening; she recounts them as embedded her experience of mainstream German society— school memories, family gatherings, and public events in her home town of Trier. Her brother, moreover, was an active member of a German youth group and later died serving the Kaiser in World War I.

This pattern of anti-Semitism in the midst of so-called normalcy makes plausible Spies's explanation of the slow Jewish reaction to the Nazi threat after Hitler came to power, even in the face of the increasing number of anti-Jewish incidents:

> It is the year 1933. At the time when the catastrophe started, a part of the Jewish people was given a certain respite. Advancing slowly, the diabolical poison gained ground only gradually. Threats and cruelties on the one hand, deceitful delays and appeasements on the other, made their victims again and again unsure, only to ultimately enmesh them in their nets more securely.[17]

For her it was clear that Jewish denial was willfully encouraged by Nazi deception.

Yet other factors also played a role. Innumerable documentary and literary portrayals of German-Jewish experiences from 1933–1945 reflect the incredulity, the indignance, and finally the anguish of those whose long-standing roots in, and service to, German society made it inconceivable to think of themselves as anything but German; their utterances prove that the acculturation that

15. Gerty Spies, *Drei Jahre Theresienstadt* (Munich: Kaiser, 1984), translated by Jutta R. Tragnitz as *My Years in Theresienstadt: How One Woman Survived the Holocaust* (Amherst, NY: Prometheus Books, 1997).

16. Spies, *Drei Jahre Theresienstadt*, 21; *My Years in Theresienstadt*, 43.

17. *My Years in Theresienstadt*, 202.

Schleiermacher and others had advocated had been internalized only too well. In his almost 1,600 pages of eye-witness account of the Hitler years, Viktor Klemperer reveals how long he persisted in his self-identification as German, not only as his national birthright but as a cultural affiliation validated by his positive contributions to society.[18]

In the words of the anonymous author of the "Political-Theological Task," Klemperer would have unquestionably considered himself among the "worthy subjects capable of civil pursuits" and thus entitled to "the many types of civil enjoyment"[19] that he did, indeed, enjoy before the Third Reich. A decorated veteran of World War I, distinguished professor of Romance languages and literatures at the Dresden Technical University, and member of the official Protestant church, Klemperer watched helplessly as Hitler's rise to power affected practicing and nonpracticing Jews alike. Although protected to some extent by virtue of his marriage to a non-Jew, the many laws and edicts aimed at the Jews deprived him of one civil right after another, ultimately threatening his very survival; he witnessed the increasingly frequent deportation and murder of individuals from the Jewish community as a daily possibility. Certainly, one major value of Klemperer's journal lies precisely in its documentation of the incremental path towards the Nazis' genocidal goals, which the victims could not foresee in detail amidst the constantly shifting landscape of new decrees and policies, but whose contours became chillingly clear along the way.

Similar to many other German Jews, Klemperer at first actively rejected, then half-heartedly pursued, efforts to emigrate, but by then it was already too late. Besides weighing the practical uncertainties of leaving the country, he simply could not conceive of any other setting for his professional and personal interests than Germany; his emotional ties to his German identity persisted as the only image of himself he could entertain. But as he saw Germany's humanistic legacy continuously undermined in the

18. Viktor Klemperer, *Ich will Zeugnis ablegen bis zum letzten: Tagebücher 1933–41*, 2 vols. (Berlin: Aufbau, 1995), slightly abridged version translated into English by Martin Chalmers, *Victor Klemperer, I Will Bear Witness: A Diary of the Nazi Years 1933–1941* (New York: Random House, 1998).

19. "Political-Theological Task," 34.

increasingly lethal measures against Jews, his ties weakened;[20] he began to see the root causes in the Germans themselves, not just in the Nazis, and he felt alienated and essentially stateless.[21] Klemperer eventually renounced and denounced all things German, if not in exchange for an unequivocal assumption of Jewish identity (which he still regarded as problematical), then at least in solidarity with the Jewish community as a *Not- und Leidensgemeinschaft*, a community of fellow sufferers through whom he discovered new dimensions of his own Jewish heritage.

The Post-1945 Legacy of Hereditary Citizenship

Spies and Klemperer survived the war and continued to reside among Germans, Spies in Munich, the Federal Republic of Germany and Klemperer in Dresden, the German Democratic Republic. Remarkably, neither of the two German states founded after the Allied defeat of Germany, despite their very different histories of dealing with the Nazi heritage, rejected or reformed the principle of hereditary citizenship that the Third Reich had adopted from the 1913 German citizenship law.[22] That legislation had allowed naturalization only "as an exception made contingent on full cultural assimilation" and "repudiation of previous citizenship."[23] Indeed, it was to the advantage of the Federal Republic, which claimed sovereignty over citizens of the German Democratic Republic as well, to emphasize that hereditary Germans belonged to one nation, if not to one state; the Federal Republic granted automatic citizenship to all GDR refugees.[24]

20. Klemperer, *Ich will Zeugnis ablegen*, 1: 340, 381, 383.

21. *Ibid.*: 340, 379, 383, 388, 411.

22. See also Bade (38–45) for a detailed description of the five phases in the postwar immigration and integration process in Germany.

23. William A. Barbieri, Jr., *Ethics of Citizenship: Immigration and Group Rights in Germany* (Durham, NC: Duke University Press, 1998), 26 (quoted from Adelson xvi and 104 n.24).

24. For further articulation of the issue, see Neuman, 263, where he remarks: "The Federal Republic maintained a legal claim to continuity with the predecessor German Empire. It never recognized East Germany as a foreign state and always regarded the citizens of East Germany as sharing a common nationality with West Germans." (quoted in Adelson, xviii).

Whereas the heredity-based citizenship of 1913 had among other things been conceived as a way to keep ties to emigrating Germans, it now functioned as one of the Cold War tools meant to undermine the GDR's hold on its residents.[25] In the GDR itself, as David Horrocks and Eva Kolinsky remark, "state policy had proclaimed internationalism, but did not allow migration of any kind."[26]

The influx of guest workers into the Federal Republic, beginning in the 1950s, added to the quandary of incorporating a sizable non-German element into an ostensibly homogenous citizenry, the so-called resettlers (*Aussiedler*). The labor treaty signed between the Federal Republic and Turkey in October 1961 was only one of the legal arrangements among those initiated since 1955, although the drastic reduction of new labor from East Germany after the building of the Berlin Wall (August 13, 1961) gave added motivation to the influx of Turkish workers. However, the governmental expectations that foreign workers would stay for a year and then return to their country of origin were quickly abandoned, in part because of the economic disadvantages of rapid worker turnover. The initial social and psychological problems posed by having a mainly male foreign work force, separated from wives and children, soon gave way to issues such as housing and schooling for foreign nationals, as families joined the men and children were born in Germany. After the guest-worker program officially ended in 1973, the Federal Republic's incentives for foreign nationals to leave were only marginally effective; guest workers had become immigrants with aspirations for permanent residency and citizenship. However, it should still be noted that between 1950 and 1995 an estimated 28 million guest workers arrived in Germany and some 20 million left.[27]

Moreover, until the 1999 citizenship law, the Federal Republic of Germany's interpretation of *ius sanguinis* promoted a curious

25. See also Kürsat-Ahlers and Waldhoff, 3.

26. David Horrocks and Eva Kolinsky, *Turkish Culture in German Society Today* (Providence, RI: Berghahn Books, 1996), xvi.

27. Dieter Dettke, "Germany's New Immigration Policy," Hearing on Germany of the Congressional Human Rights Caucus, Thursday, Oct. 11, 2001:2, <www.fesdc.org/dcbio.htm>. For a more extensive treatment of *Gastarbeiter* policies and issues, see Neuman 247–97; also see Horrocks and Kolinsky.

double standard for foreigners in Germany: The government sponsored so-called repatriation for thousands of Eastern Europeans of German descent. These resettlers (*Aussiedler*) had never lived in Germany and often spoke no German but could document a German ancestor—in many cases fraudulently. As Klaus Bade notes, due to generous integration programs not given to other immigrants, "the ethnic Germans from the East still are by far the most privileged immigrant group in Germany."[28] At the same time pre-1999 citizenship policy excluded from automatic naturalization German-born children of migrants, who were already culturally integrated; it stipulated a fifteen-year residency to qualify for German citizenship, somewhat reminiscent of some 1799 proposals for a lengthy period of civil education or probation for people already raised in the midst of German language and culture. Indeed, it looked as if the Federal Government's migration policy would continue to prevent "a long-term population from rights of participation for the foreseeable future"[29]

A Multi-Ethnic Germany: Accomplishments and Ongoing Obstacles

Fortunately, the reform of the citizenship laws in 1999 has basically removed the most significant cause of such a prognosis. Numerous official and societal efforts have been undertaken to implement the law and overcome psychological and cultural barriers to meaningful integration of resident foreigners, whether citizens or not. Nonetheless, since the law went into effect, there has been a veritable zigzag course pitting attempts to achieve more finely tuned policies for the entry of foreigners and their integration against opponents of immigration, asylum, and recognition of a multiethnic culture.

The very definition of integration, with opinions ranging from acculturation to assimilation, has repeatedly been the subject of political discussion. The duty has often fallen on the non-nationals themselves to fit into German society, rather on efforts of the majority society to promote integration; discrimination

28. Bade, 40.
29. Kürsat-Ahlers and Waldhoff, 4.

and barriers remain in the fields of housing, health, and employ-
ment.[30] Even as a government commission appointed in 2000
began to work on new legislative initiatives for immigration and
integration policy, a debate about requiring acceptance of the
German *Leitkultur* ("defining culture") as a condition for further
immigration and asylum coursed through the Bundestag and in
the press for several weeks of fall 2000, leaving its mark on all
subsequent debates.[31] The 1999 citizenship law already requires
that candidates for citizenship have a satisfactory command of
the German language. Beyond that, however, proponents of the
Leitkultur nation argued that residents of foreign origin should
adapt their ways to the basic customs and values of the majority
culture (i.e., Christian values and German habits and customs).
No wonder that many Turks are wary of integration as "nothing
short of absolute assimilation, the disappearance of Anatolian
faces behind German masks,"[32] a demand recalling some of the
assumptions about Jewish assimilation to Christian culture
voiced in the 1799 debate. Given the guarantee of human rights
in the German constitution, the politicians should do well to
remember Schleiermacher's observation that one can't be forbidden to do anything related to religion that is allowed by the
state (103).

Beyond the sheer difficulty of achieving official definitions,
however, the debate revealed the underlying fears that ethnic
diversity would dilute the supposedly homogeneous German culture; it simultaneously reinforced negative stereotypes. Yet, as
pointed out by Dieter Dettke, executive director of the Washington
office of the Friedrich Ebert Foundation, even the most cursory

30. European Commission against Racism and Intolerance, "CRI (2001) 36 Second Report on Germany," *Council of Europe*, adopted December 15, 2000, made
public July 3, 2001: 10, 2 (hereafter referred to as ECRI). <http://www.coe.int/T/
E/human_rights/Ecri/1-ECRI/2-Country-by-country_approach/Germany/
Germany_CBC_2.asp#TopOfPage>.

31. The issue was raised in October by Christian Democratic Representative
Friedrich Merz, who took the term from his Bavarian colleague, Günter Bechstein.
See also Dieter Oberndörfer, "Was ist eigentlich ein integrierter Deutscher? Zur
Debatte über die 'Leitkultur', die Gewährung von Asyl und Zuwanderung sowie
die Integration von Ausländern" in *Frankfurter Rundschau online*, October 24, 2000:
5, <www.fr-aktuell.de/fr/spezial/auslaender/t2024073.htm>.

32. "Germany: Home for Turks?" in Şenocak, 6.

overview of German history indicates an intermingling with many different ethnic groups, including the Slavs, the Dutch, and the French Huguenots,[33] but also going back to the contacts of the Germanic tribes with the Romans and the Celts. Cultural homogeneity has always been, as Dieter Oberndörfer notes, only fictitious and stands in the way of cultural pluralism.[34]

The statistics alone would argue that Germany is already a multiethnic society. In 2000, the number of legal resident foreigners was almost 7.3 million, which comprised 8.9 percent of the total population, with 1.5 million non-Germans born in Germany. The roughly 2 million Turkish citizens (some sources list a higher figure[35]) constituted the largest minority group, with 750,000 born in Germany. These figures do not include another 425,000 Turks who had been naturalized since 1972.[36] Of course, many politicians—and their constituents—have continually seen the high numbers of foreigners and a high German unemployment rate as a reason to resist further immigration and liberalization of asylum procedures. However, Dieter Oberndörfer points to cases where the failure to cite the numbers of foreigners who have left the country alongside the numbers of immigrants has created an exaggerated picture of a so-called flood of immigrants and asylum-seekers.[37] More telling statistics reveal that at the end of 1999, 32 percent of the total migrant population had lived in Germany for twenty years or longer, 40 percent for more than fifteen years, and 52 percent for more than ten years."[38] As the second and third generations grow up in Germany, their permanent presence is an undisputable reality.

33. Dettke, 1.

34. Dieter Oberndörfer speaks of "die immer nur fiktiv gewesene kulturelle Homogenität" in "Was ist eigentlich ein integrierter Deutscher?", 1.

35. For example, "Immigranten: Deutsche Heimat," in Der Spiegel 25 (June 16) 2001: 17, reported 2.4 million.

36. Veysel Oezcan, "Germany: Immigration in Transition," Migration Policy Institute, May 2002: 5, <http://www.migrationinformation.org/Feature/display.cfm?ID=515>.

37. Dieter Oberndorfer (4) mentions remarks in 2000 by Interior Minister Otto Schily and Bavarian Minister Beckstein relating to 1998 figures.

38. ECRI, 10. The Commission's report points out that these figures are diluted by the "relatively large influx of asylum seekers and refugees over the last decade and the short 'length of stay' of migrant children born in Germany."

Meanwhile, statistics also reveal the impact that a declining birthrate, an aging populace, and competition in the world market had on the serious shortage of skilled technical workers, especially in the field of information technology; the change in demographics also presents problems for financing social security programs. Realizing the urgent need for immediate practical solutions, the Social Democratic (SDP)-Greens coalition government introduced a green card system in August 2000 as a stopgap measure; it provided for streamlined admission of 20,000 qualified participants per year, each allowed to work in Germany for five years.[39] Even with just 13,000 German green cards issued by February 2003, the program has been seen as highly effective.[40] Nonetheless, the program will end on July 31, 2003, in part because it was supposed to give way to a more comprehensive legislative action.

Indeed, by 2001 the major political parties were united in their recognition of the need for a more finely tuned policy for dealing with the entry of foreigners. The government-appointed commission's report in July 2001, titled "Structuring Immigration, Fostering Immigration," argued for "initiating a controlled immigration program for foreigners with favorable characteristics for integration into both the labor market and society;"[41] it included provisions for asylum procedures and for integration of immigrants. By the end of 2001 the government presented a "Draft Law for the Management and Limitation of Immigration and for the Regulation of the Abode and Integration of Citizens of the European Union as well as Foreigners." In spite of its somewhat awkward language, this proposed immigration law (*Zuwanderungsgesetz*) represented, in the words of Dieter Dettke, "a fundamental change of German Immigration policy. Germany's identity, from now on, will be that of a country of immigration."[42] The proposed law provided a set of criteria for the

---

39. In its provisions, this green card actually more closely resembles the United States' H1-B visa than its permanent green card. Participation also requires a university- or college-level degree. See Dieter Dettke, "Germany's New Immigration Policy."

40. "German Green Card programme to end after 31st July 2003," *Workpermit.com*, February 2003, <http://www.workpermit.com/news/germany7.htm>. Indian nationals have been the largest single group.

41. Oezcan, 7.

42. Dettke, 1.

admission of immigrants that would simplify and streamline the categories of work and residency permits.

At the same time, as Dettke acknowledges, this "demand-oriented concept implies that there are both opportunities and limits related to the labor market conditions at any given time.[43] Namely, it would give priority to highly skilled workers with job offers, to scientific specialists, to graduates of German universities, and to entrepreneurs, as well as provide educational and administrative measures to promote integration.[44] A later statement by Interior Minister Schily, meant to reassure citizens concerned about the impact of foreigners on the labor market, reveals the law's limits: "Foreign applicants will only get a chance in areas where the German workforce is lacking." In other words, the law favors so-called useful foreigners; companies cannot hire migrant workers who are not considered highly skilled unless there are no Germans or European Union nationals to fill the job.[45] The law also tightens asylum rules, providing for only a temporary three-year residence permit unless verifiable requirements warrant permanent residency.[46] Nonetheless, taken as a whole, the provisions would make the German immigration system "probably the most liberal in Europe."[47]

Yet the law, which was supposed to go into effect on January 1, 2003, has suffered several setbacks. Passed by both the Parliament Lower House (*Bundestag*) and the Parliament Upper House (*Bundesrat*) by early March 2002 and signed in June 2002

43. Dettke, 6.

44. Those provisions that ultimately were adopted included 1) immediate and unlimited residency for highly skilled workers and scientific specialists with valid job offers; 2) by 2010 a points-based system similar to Canada's for skilled workers without job offers; 3) combined residence and work permit; 4) an extendable one-year residence permit for foreign graduates of German universities; 5) compulsory integration courses for new migrants on language, history, culture, and the German constitution; and 6) creation of a federal office for migration and refugees and a migration council. See "Germany to Liberalize Immigration," *workpermit.com*, August 3, 2001 <http://www.workpermit.com/news/germany7.htm> and Oezcan, "Germany: Immigration in Transition," as well as Oezcan, "German Immigration Law Clears Final Hurdle," in *Migration Policy Institute*, September 1, 2002, <http://www.migrationinformation.org/Feature/display.cfm?ID=51>.

45. Oezcan, "Germany: Immigration in Transition," 7.

46. Oezcan, "German Immigration Law," 3.

47. "Germany: Delays to New Immigration Law," *Workpermit.com*, 4.

House (*Bundesrat*) by early March 2002 and signed in June 2002 by President Johannes Rau, the Constitutional Court (*Bundesver-fassungsgericht*) declared the *Bundesrat* passage void on December 23, 2002, because of an improperly cast vote. The Federal cabinet reintroduced the draft law in March 2003, but on June 20, 2003, the CDU/CSU majority in the *Bundesrat*, citing the lack of major changes in its provisions, rejected it once more.[48] After the vote, Premier Peter Müller of Saarland explained: "It's not about hindering immigration, but about limiting immigration. The law doesn't allow for that and that's why it's not acceptable"[49] and cited as the reason Germany's high unemployment rate.[50] Indeed, after a brief downturn, figures stood in June 2003 at 4.453 million, or 10.7 percent of the workforce.[51] It appeared that even many of the immigrant holders of the green card are among those who have become unemployed.[52] Interior Minister Schily countered that the danger to jobs was a legend, as his draft included the kind of guidance and limitation the CDU had demanded.[53] The bill was sent to the parliamentary mediation committee whose working group has continued to seek an acceptable compromise that can be presented to the upper house in March 2004.[54]

Whatever the eventual shape of the law, both sides at least agree about the necessity of regulating immigration and modernizing laws governing foreigners. The German economy, already under

48. "Germans Reject Sweeping Immigration Law," in *Deutsche Welle*, June 20, 2003, <http://www.dw-world.de/english/0,3367,1432_A_898151_1_A,00.html>.

49. "Germans Reject Sweeping Immigration Law," *Deutsche Welle*, June 20, 2003. "The opposition Christian Democratic Union and its Bavarian sister party, the Christian Social Union, who hold a majority in the Bundesrat, refused to approve the bill, complaining Schily had made no changes. . . . The Union parties have made no less than 128 proposals for change to the bill."

50. Lukas Wallraff, "Union bremst Zuwanderung," *die tageszeitung*, June 21, 2003: 7, <http://www.taz.de/pt/2003/06/21/a0009.nf/text>.

51. "German unemployment in first fall for 15 months," *The Guardian World News*, June 5, 2003, <http://www.guardian.co.uk/germany/article/0,2763, 970941,00.html>.

52. "Study Shows Many German Green Card Holders out of Work," *Deutsche Welle*, June 17, 2003, <http://www.dw-world.de/english/0,3367, 1430_A_895404, 00.html>.

53. Wallraff, 7.

54. <http://www.bundesregierung.de/en>.

laws governing foreigners. The German economy, already under the stress of a possible recession, cannot afford to ignore the realities of the labor shortage and global competition. Moreover, progress in changing everyday attitudes towards foreigners and minorities lacks momentum until implementation of new immigration and asylum laws can help foster acceptance of a heterogeneous citizenry by the populace at large.

In anticipation of the 2002 immigration law, at least one official reinforcement of such efforts took effect: The new Federal Office for Immigration and Refugees was officially opened on July 1, 2002, and charged with "providing the necessary institutional support for immigrants by the federal government, and active participation of immigrants in these programs."[55] The centerpiece of its duties, if funded as planned, is the development of the federally financed integration courses for foreigners and ethnic German resettlers, including language courses and basic courses on German law, culture, and history.[56] Beyond the obvious benefits for foreigners, however, the mandatory nature of the course also raises once more the issues of assimilation versus acculturation that reverberated in the *Leitkultur* debate. The call for migrants to adapt to the dominant culture must be matched by meaningful encouragement of cultural and ethnic pluralism in the majority society. As ECRI observes, it is necessary to recognize "the positive contribution made by individuals of foreign origin."[57]

In the meantime, lack of the full range of legal instruments can hamper progress in overcoming the fundamental barriers noted by the European Commission against Racism and Intolerance. In its 2001 report on Germany it still can state about migrants:

> These individuals, even those who are the second or third generation born in Germany, remain migrants or foreigners in German statistics, public discourse and life. The concept and usage of the term "foreigner" seems sometimes to encompass an even larger group

55. ECRI, 6.

56. "Immigration and Refugees Officially Opened," *Federal Government*, Tuesday, July 7, 2002, <http://eng.bundesregierung.de/top/dokumente/Artikel/ix_15440.htm?template=single&id=15440_7080&script=1&ixepf=_15440_7080>.

57. ECRI, 2.

of the population, also including those minorities who have lived for many generations in Germany.[58]

The reality registered in language, then, still reveals the self-perpetuating circle of foreigners producing foreigners; it has, to some extent, been legally breached but not psychologically dissolved. The ECRI's words also imply that the attitudes towards foreigners extend even to citizens from minority groups with at least partial ties to the ethnic German heritage, such as Afro-Germans and Jewish Germans. Any efforts to internalize the spirit of actual and pending legislation permit no illusions about the insidious and virulent confluence of xenophobia, racism, and anti-Semitism that undercut efforts at integration and acceptance.

To some extent, it was the political events of 1989, culminating in the reunification of Germany in 1990, that unleashed racist and xenophobic violence held in check by the political dynamics of the two Germanys.[59] Furthermore, such attacks have in part been linked to the disproportionate effects that high unemployment, rising inflation, and fears about the future had in the former Eastern Germany, complicated by the existence of neo-Nazi organizations.[60]

However, such factors alone cannot explain the ongoing virulence of the phenomenon. Despite countless citizen demonstrations in the 1990s against these violent, xenophobic acts and despite more effective measures taken by the SDP-Greens coalition after winning the 1998 election, the ECRI report notes as of December 2000:

> Racist and anti-Semitic violence is one of the most pressing and dangerous expressions of racism and

58. ECRI, 10.

59. It has been argued that the Federal Republic upheld the old citizenship laws during the years of two Germanys to underscore its claim to represent Germans in both states; after reunification the leading Christian Democratic Party did not pursue revisions in citizenship law, despite the risks of "ethnization," out of concern that liberalization would feed the growing nationalism. See Kürsat-Ahlers and Waldhoff, 1.

60. ECRI, 10. Also, Şenocak notes in 1995 that "four thousand to five thousand attacks and transgressions against 'foreigners' (*Fremde*) take place annually. ("Thoughts on May 8, 1995," in *Atlas of a Tropical Germany*, 60). See also Horrocks and Kolinsky, "Introduction" xvi–xvii, for the psychological aspects of prejudice and xenophobia after unification.

intolerance in Germany. There are frequent reports of harassment and attacks, some resulting in death, against members of minority groups, who are afraid to appear in public in certain regions of the country. These attacks are aimed at individuals of foreign [ancestry] as well as members of the Jewish community. Visible minorities are particularly susceptible to such attacks.[61]

The conflation of anti-Semitism with xenophobia and racism is particularly troubling in its implications for the entrenchment and intransigency of the problems. For even though the number of actual perpetrators and their active supporters is relatively small, ECRI says that it may represent a much more widespread, latent sympathy in all parts of Germany, not just the former GDR; such high-profile acts, as such, "may be viewed as an extreme manifestation of a broader climate of racism, anti-Semitism, and intolerance"[62] This broader climate must be understood if it is to be changed.

The aforementioned analysis of ethnic essentialism by Kürsat-Ahlers and Hans-Peter Waldhoff already provides some insight. Other voices contribute perspectives on the roots of xenophobia and racism. Pondering the link between violence against foreigners and the issue of German identity, East German author Christa Wolf wonders "out of what depths of the German soul these eruptions of hate and violence come, with which every kind of injury to an unbelievably weak self-identity are answered in Germany?"[63] The ECRI pinpoints one factor as "the lack of recognition of the possibility that German identity may also be associated with other forms of identity than the traditional one."[64] Probing deeper, Zafer Ṣenocak analyzes the phenomenon as a crisis of identity in the wake of the Cold War. He observes a dissolution of the individual subject ("our self-image turns out to be a fiction"), but also "a confusion and disorientation regarding the collective identity, especially when the illusion

61. ECRI, 11.

62. ECRI, 12.

63. Christa Wolf, "Begegnung Third Street," Hierzulande-Andernorts (Munich: Luchterhand, 1999), 35.

64. ECRI, 2.

of homogeneity breaks down."[65] Thus identity, as "an idea born of lack," is driven by the need "to create that homogeneity synthetically, an order founded on purging the Other,[66] on annihilation of differences."[67]

Nor is this phenomenon exclusively German, says Şenocak. Besides the most recent conflicts in the former Yugoslavia and the Caucasus, France's war in the 1950s with Algeria and its aftermath, and even the colonial history of the British Empire, the efforts of the European Union exhibit aspects of the phenomenon: "Europe at the close of the twentieth century is a very insecure, deeply divided continent, which is playing an elaborate unification game to repress its own contradictions and conflicts."[68] His analysis would apply all too aptly to many other societies in the world as well.

Given the ongoing potential for violence that resides in the unacknowledged and unreconstructed projections of one's own fears and prejudices onto the Other, Şenocak argues that authentic communication about the issue requires us to "confront our consciousness with what comes out of our unconscious."[69] This phenomenon affects migrants as well as the majority society: "They demonize the Other in themselves and themselves in the other."[70]

Beyond the psychoanalytical dimension of the task, Şenocak also speaks quite practically of the need to learn from causes and consequences in German history: "Only then will we understand what resistance there is in Germany today towards immigrants."[71] He discovers, in analyzing the history of Jews in Germany, an

65. "War and Peace in Modernity," in Şenocak, 84.

66. "The Other" is Adelson's translation of the term *das Fremde*, which, as she notes, can mean "foreign" as well as "strange" and thus overlaps in some contexts with associated words such as *der Fremde* ("the stranger") and *Ausländer* ("foreigner"). Both circles of words have connotations that "reinforce the misperception that people who ostensibly 'look different' are in fact not Germans," whether or not they are legal citizens ("Coordinates of Orientation," in Şenocak, xxxvi).

67. Şenocak, "War and Peace," 85.

68. *Ibid.*, 86. On the British Empire, see Şenocak, "'Orient' and 'Occident,'" in *Atlas of a Tropical Germany*, 17.

69. Şenocak, "War and Peace," 97.

70. *Ibid.*, 85.

71. Karin Yeşilada, in an interview with Zafer Şenocak, "May One Compare Turks and Jews, Mr. Şenocak?" in *Atlas of a Tropical Germany*, 53.

experiential background that is particularly useful for the Turks, encompassing

> the creative influence that this history had (but also the effect of Enlightenment on Jews, with all its consequences, including emancipation and assimilation). . . . Even the bitter experiences that led to the [near] annihilation of the Jewish minority in Europe must be reflected upon in the conception of a multicultural Europe.[72]

Careful not to set up any simplistic comparisons, Şenocak emphasizes the time differential involved, as the experience of the Jews in Germany extended over a thousand years, compared to the short time span for the Turks since 1961.[73]

Despite this postscript's emphasis on the primacy of ethnic essentialism, any reference to possible parallels between Turks and Jews must include the role of religion, so crucial in the 1799 debates. With over 3 million Muslims today in Germany, religion once more proves its relevance as "a line of separation" between the majority and minority society,[74] all the more so because Germany, unlike other EU countries, does not recognize Islam as a legitimate religious community.[75] The presence in Germany of foreign political and religious associations, some with their own irrational and exclusionary politics, has raised thorny problems, even before the terrorist attacks on September 11, 2001. Since that momentous event, the discovery of the involvement of Islamic students in Hamburg with the terrorist cell connected to the strategic planning of the attack on the World Trade Center has led to revisions in the religious privilege of foreign associations.[76] The

72. Şenocak, "Germany—Home for Turks?" 6.

73. Yeşilada (54) where Şenocak remarks, "A society dominated by a social majority regards the "Others" as foreign (*Fremde*), as not belonging. Above all, religion marks a line of separation."

74. http://www.cia.gov/cia/publications/factbook/.

75. Şenocak, "Germany–Home for Turks?" 8.

76. Dettke, 5. See also an evaluation of the situation six months after 9/11: Dieter Dettke, "Sechs Monate nach dem 11. September: Eine Zwischenbilanz," *Friedrich Ebert Foundation,* report for the SPD faction of the Bundestag, March 6, 2002, <http://www.fesdc.org/DD%20Speeches%20+%20Articles/Zwischenbilanz%2011.September.html>.

tendency world-wide to conflate terrorists and Islam threatens to affirm a question Şenocak posed rhetorically in 1990: "But doesn't anti-Islam, dug out of medieval mothballs and restyled for the present, threaten to join the anti-Semitism of European history?"[77] Although not all Turks are Muslim, the Western world all too often fuses ethnicity, religion, and appearance in one monolithic stereotype.

Beyond Xenophobia and Violence to Integration and Tolerance

Given the tenor of the times, then, it is hard to predict what it might take to keep up momentum towards a truly multicultural society, in Germany or elsewhere. As Şenocak remarks: "Integration is not achieved when the differences of others are used to consolidate one's own image of the world."[78] His advice to Turks and Germans alike still seems relevant, namely, to recognize and embrace heterogeneity in a world that "is not marked by a chasm, but by many visible and invisible fissures that simultaneously divide us and link us together."[79] He encourages encounters in which the cultural dimensions of otherness are discussed meaningfully, with listening to the other and entering the world of the other, "that, like one's own, is also determined by heritage and memory."[80] In this regard, all sectors of society must be encouraged to think as citizens, not with the nationalistic fervor of the tribe, but sharing with hereditary Germans a "constitutional patriotism" stressing common civil rights and values that engenders a nonethnic view of what it means to be German.[81] To accomplish this goal, Şenocak challenges the majority and the minority cultures to create a "new shared language," which is his

77. Şenocak, "Germany–Home for Turks?" 6.

78. Şenocak, "War and Peace," 93.

79. Şenocak, "Which Myth Writes Me?" in *Atlas of a Tropical Germany*, 82.

80. Şenocak, "War and Peace," 95, 96.

81. Şenocak,"What Does the Forest Dying Have to Do with Multiculturalism?" in *Atlas of a Tropical Germany*, 25. Leslie Adelson notes that the term "constitutional patriotism" stems from the political social philosophy of Jürgen Habermas of the Frankfurt School of Critical Theory (123, n.2).

shorthand for a genuine, exploratory discourse to chart the common territory shared by both.[82] It would foster complex conversation and substantive knowledge of the Other that gets beyond preconceived opinions and identities; such a language could facilitate a fruitful contact (*Berührung*) that would allow something new to grow.[83]

This fruitful contact has begun to take concrete shape over the last decade in ways that may yet mean true progress. ECRI noted favorably in its 2001 report the various initiatives in democratic education carried out by the federal and regional centers for political education, "which include measures aimed at reducing prejudice and xenophobia [as well as those promoting] an appreciation of cultural diversity within vocational training in certain Länder."[84]

One major force for such initiatives has been the Alliance for Democracy and Tolerance (*Bündnis für Demokratie und Toleranz*), created in May 2000 by the German government as an "umbrella for political activities involving political actors as well as actors of civil society and the private sphere."[85] Its programs are intended

> to address right-wing extremism . . . and to work with determination for the protection and respect of democratic rules, for respect of the dignity of man, as well as for tolerance and solidarity. . . . [It is] committed to working against xenophobia and violence as well as against undemocratic, extremist or xenophobic behaviour.[86]

In one example of its work, the Dresdner Bank, which "considers promoting democracy and humanity to be one of its primary tasks," joined the Second German Television network (ZDF) and Alliance for Democracy to launch the "Victor Klemperer Youth

82. Şenocak, "The Concept of Culture and its Discontents," in *Atlas of a Tropical Germany*, 46.

83. *Ibid.*, 43, 47–8.

84. ECRI, 13.

85. *Ibid.*

86. "Alliance for Democracy and Tolerance: Initiative against Extremism and Violence," *Federal Government*, August 11, 2000, <http://www.bundesregierung.de/en/Latest-News/Information-from-the-Governmen-,10157.15440/artikel/Alliance-for-Democracy-and-Tol.htm>.

Competition for Democracy and Tolerance," an annual essay competition with prizes.[87] The Alliance also sponsors annual "Democracy and Tolerance" prizes, worth between 1,000 and 5,000 euros. In 2003, the Alliance gave prizes to 89 projects (out of 300 submitted), with the highest awarded to "Action: Courage" for a project to integrate Muslims in Germany that is "leading the way in bringing together Muslim organizations and social services . . . " Also noted was the organization's cooperation with the Municipal Prevention Council, which works together with the Youth Office, police, schools, and street workers to help at-risk youths from immigrant Muslim families.[88] In addition to the responsible federal ministries, there are now more than 200 initiatives, organizations and individuals involved in the Alliance, such as AKTIONCOURAGE (Project Courage), Pro Asyl, and the Turkish Community in Germany (*Türkische Gemeinde in Deutschland*).[89]

Without playing down the considerable barriers to a truly functional, multicultural society in Germany, there are indications that a multicultural society, in however imperfect form, has already changed the cultural countenance of the country; residents and citizens with non-German names increasingly garner titles such as "Best National Artist" and [best] "Youth Researchers in North-Rheinland-Westphalia," or hold positions as news anchor or win world championships.[90] Such anecdotal assessments of integration are bolstered by a 2001 survey conducted for the German federal government and reported in the magazine *Der Spiegel* showing that 56 percent of the resident Turks are well integrated and that 24 percent have "integration potential." Of

87. "Victor Klemperer Youth Competition 2002/2003: Germany: What's That?" *Dresdner Bank.com*, <http://www.dresdnerbank.com/content/03_unternehmen/05_gesellschaftliches_engagement/09_viktor.html>.

88. From the speech of the chairman of the Bundestag's Internal Affairs Committee, Cornelie Sonntag-Wolgast (SPD), *German News* (English Edition) Wednesday, March 26, 2003, <http://www.mathematik.uni-ulm.de/de-news/2003/03/261800.html#9>.

89. See AKTIONCOURAGE, <http://www.aktioncourage.org/>, Pro Asyl, <http://www.proasyl.de/>, Interkultureller Rat, <http://www.interkulturellerrat.de/ >, and Türkische Gemeinde in Deutschland, <http://www.tgd.de/>.

90. Examples from a statement by a deputy of the Federal German government, quoted by Kürsat-Ahlers and Waldhoff, 4.

the 20 percent that are poorly integrated, most are women and male senior citizens, but 80 percent of Turkish youth regularly meet German friends.[91] Such figures balance the anecdotal evidence about the problems of young male Turks searching for ways to assert their power in ways that get beyond the macho behavior.

Finally, the role of the churches in fostering integration marks a significant change from the time of the 1799 debate. In a speech from January 2003, Manfred Kock, the chairperson of the Council of the Evangelical Church in Germany (EKD), reviewed the specific contributions German churches have made to the integration of migrants and refugees from the time of the first *Gastarbeiter*. They not only have furthered discussions and sponsored concrete assistance, but also have repeatedly called for legal action and legislative reforms to preserve and extend the fundamental rights guaranteed by the Basic Law, which functions as Germany's constitution.[92] Among other things, Kock underscores the two-fold implication of the ecumenical work of the EKD and the Council of Catholic Bishops. In addition to inter-Christian understanding, their efforts have fostered many significant inter-faith initiatives among Christians and other religions, mindful of the validity of the Gospel's message for all people, regardless of national, ethnic, linguistic, and cultural heritage.

Moreover, Kock regards the Ecumenical Council of Churches' principle of "unity in reconciled diversity" (*Einheit in versöhnter Verschiedenheit*) as a model for integration that can and must be transposed to secular life: Germany's Basic Law, as the legal framework for the rights and obligations of all people living in Germany, must be accepted as binding for the social formation of a society where the expressions of cultural plurality are respected and supported. Integration must not mean faceless assimilation but the right to preserve and develop one's cultural identity as long as it is consistent with the Basic Law. Kock welcomes the

91. "Immigranten: Deutsche Heimat," *Der Spiegel* No. 25 (June 18), 2001: 17. The survey was conducted by the communications scholar Hans-Jürgen Weiss with the GKF Television Research of Nuremburg and the media institute Göfak.

92. Manfred Kock, "Zuwanderung und Integration aus kirchlicher Sicht," *Evangelische Kirche in Deutschland*, January 31, 2003, <http://www.ekd.de/vor-traege/154_030131_kock_zuwanderung.html>.

Islamic Charter, issued in February 2002 by the Central Committee of Muslims in Germany, for its endorsement of the federal government's basic democratic principles, including human rights and religious freedom. Yet he expressed concern about the ambiguities in such areas as Islamic women's rights and the renunciation of an Islamic state. He insists that the Islamic offer for discussion and cooperation must be followed by concrete engagement of all parties, with the realization that conflict resolution and true integration involve a long-term process.[93]

This concrete engagement of all parties is already part of the agenda of the International Council of Christians and Jews (ICCJ), which for fifty years has promoted Jewish-Christian relations. Through its thirty-eight national Jewish-Christian dialog organizations, the ICCJ "offers a platform where people of different religious backgrounds examine current issues across national and religious boundaries, enabling face-to-face exchanges of experience and expertise."[94] From its headquarters at the Martin Buber House in Heppenheim, Germany, it sponsors a wide range of conferences and programs; it provides a meeting place for scholars and students engaged in interreligious projects.[95] Both the ICCJ and the Martin Buber House issue newsletters and other publications.[96]

Responding to the growing significance of Islam in Western European countries, the ICCJ also established in 1995 the Abrahamic Forum Council, with the goal of applying the successful approaches of the Christian-Jewish interactions to a "trilateral" dialog among Jews, Christians, and Muslims.[97] At the opening of

93. Manfred Kock, "Zuwanderung und Integration aus kirchlicher Sicht." Further details of the EKD's position on the Islamic Charter appear in "Stellungnahme des Kirchenamtes der Evangelischen Kirche in Deutschland zu der vom Zentralrat der Muslime in Deutschland e.V. vorgelegten 'Islamischen Charta,'" *Evangelische Kirche Deutschland,* January 2003, <http://www.ekd.de/EKD-Texte/2078_islam_charta2003.html>.

94. ICCJ, home page statement, <http://www.iccj.org/en/index.php>.

95. "Die Geschichte des Martin Buber-Hauses, <http://www.iccj.org/en/displayItem.php?id=166>.

96. *ICCJ Newsletter* and the *Martin-Buber-Haus Rundbrief.*

97. Friedhelm Pieper, "Abrahamic Forum Council—Opening and Welcome," First Conference of the ICCJ Abrahamic Forum Council: Berlin, Germany, October 21–4, 1999, <http://www.iccj.org/en/displayItem.php?id=109>.

the first AFC conference in Berlin in 1999, Friedhelm Pieper, General Secretary of the ICCJ, stressed that the efforts to overcome demonization of the Other, to find "common and authentic ways to express differences without causing offense," and to resolve conflicts require a multilevel approach: at the grass-root level of the neighborhoods, among religious leaders, through education, and in politics and administration of government at all levels.[98]

The complex paths of cause and effect, action and reaction, allow no easy judgments of past actors, but they do allow some intriguing comparisons. Schleiermacher faulted the Prussian state for its inaction regarding emancipation of the Jews, but also speculated about the ambiguities and a possible subtext in Friedländer's proposals; Teller could or would only give the Jewish householders his advice about the path to Christianity but not his assessment of their bid for citizenship. In contrast, the churches in the Federal Republic have contributed to a climate in which the citizenship law of 1999 could ultimately pass; indeed, Kock regards a new immigration law as long overdue and laments the roadblocks to its passage. He welcomes Interior Minister Schily's recognition of the churches' initiation of dialog with migrants along with his admission about the reciprocal dependency of church and state in working for acceptance and tolerance.[99] The Islamic Charter and the reactions to it offer an intriguing comparison to the debate about the Jewish householders' willingness to give up ceremonial law and its identity as a "nation" as part of the price of citizenship.[100] Finally, Friedhelm Pieper's response to "The Christian Faith and Non-Christian Religions," the position paper released on August 1, 2003, by Manfred Kock of the EKD, suggests parallels, but also permutations, of the Friedländer-Teller exchange concerning common features shared by Jews and Christians—for example, the role of Christ and his relevance for Jewish religious history, extending it to Muslims as well.[101]

98. *Ibid.*

99. Kock quotes a speech by Otto Schily given in September 2002 in Berlin.

100. The Charter of the Central Council of Muslims in Germany, as well as analyses and reactions, can be viewed in English at <http://www.quantara.de/>.

101. While affirming several points of Kock's position, Pieper sees missed opportunities to foster a "trilateral" rapprochement; for example: the common link through Abraham; the "unrevoked covenant" (*der ungekündigte Bund*) in the

It is possible, then, that changes in the political culture have begun to filter through the institutions of society and public consciousness. Since the major political parties finally recognize Germany as a land of immigration as well as the need for meaningful integration, further progress seems possible, if only patience and substantive progress can prevail over events that foster polarization. Many issues, such as dual citizenship and the debate about banning head scarves in schools, remain to be dealt with, in Germany as well as in the context of the European Union. The ECRI report, not known for unfounded optimism, puts the situation in perspective: "One also has to anticipate that there will be setbacks, but the struggle must be won and it will be won."[102] And one is permitted to hope that the ghosts of the thorny issues of 1799, with their long course of partial, ineffectual solutions, will finally attain, if not closure, then at least a foundation for ongoing, positive transformation of the ways a heterogeneous populace can live together.

Julie Klassen

Sinai; and the roles of Christ as rabbi and prophet, not just as redeemer. Friedhelm Pieper, "Hilfreich und problematisch zugleich: Zum EKD Papier 'Christlicher Glaube und nichtchristliche Religionen,'" August 7, 2003, International Council of Christians and Jews, >http://www.iccj.org/en/displayItem.php?id=160>. Pieper's review refers to Manfred Kock, "Christlicher Glaube und nichtchristliche Religionen. Theologische Leitlinien," a position paper of the Evangelical Church of Germany (EKD), Text 77, August 1, 2003, >http://www.ekd.de/EKD-Texte/2059_35254.html>.

102. ECRI, 8.

Index

ceremonial law, 5, 10, 15, 16, 19n.
44; cancellation of, 55, 67–8;
contrasted with ritual and
basic law, 116–8, 125, 143;
exactitude of, 42, 45, 57–9, 77;
status of, 23, 25, 26, 27, 48, 53,
84, 91, 104, 106
Charles V, 141, 144n. 75
church and state, 1, as rivals,
139–41; Augsburg Interim,
141n. 69; case of France,
99n. 40; free worship in
U.S., 141; Jefferson on, 3;
Judaism as state-recognized,
23, 28; not separated in
biblical times, 53–4; restrained
bitterness regarding, 90–1;
so-called Christian states,
85; state religion, 138–9; theo-
rists of, Benedikt Carpzov,
Justus Henning Böhmer,
139, 140; three patterns of,
137–9
citizenship, 1, 13, 23, 26, 39, 95,
96, 97, 102, 124, 125, 138, 140,
141, 145–7, 149–50; and ethnic
identity, 148; citizenship law
(1913), 4, 150, 154; citizenship
law (1999), 146, 154, 156, 171;
hereditary, 153–5; Schleiermacher's denial of religious test
for, 20, 22, 85
communion, sacrament of, 27,
129–30
Constantine the Great, 119, 138
contemporary German immigration policies, 150, 155–66
conversion of Jews, 14, 16, 17, 20,
21, 26, 28, 84, 90n. 19, 92, 94,
97n. 37, 105, 109, 123, 136, 142;
Political-Theological Task on,
34–40

deism, 8, in the *Open Letter*, 48–
51, 128n. 39; of Thomas Paine,
29, 115n. 3; *see also* truths of
reason
doctrine, 32, 33, 36, 38, 128, 130–
2; messiah as accidental, 106;
of the son of God, 75, 93–4;
Teller on New Testament basis
of, 11, 131n. 31
Dohm, Christian Wilhelm von,
*On the Civil Improvement of the
Jews*, 3
Dohna, Alexander von, 18n. 42

education, as self-formation, 97n.
36; Friedländer on Jewish
path in, 42–7; in the Enlightenment, 1, 5, 10–1, 15, 33, 48–
9, 88n. 17; Jewish free school
in Berlin, 5; of Jews compared
to Christians, 62–3, 99; of Jews
for citizenship, 14, 22, 38–9,
155; *see also* Teller and
Haskalah
Essenes, 26, 122
Euchel, Isaac Abraham, 26, 121n.
19
European Commission on Racism and Intolerance (ECRI),
156n. 30, 157n. 38, 161–3, 167,
172
European Union, 158, 159, 164,
172

French Huguenots, 103n. 48, 157
French Revolution, 24n. 52, 29,
99n. 40
Friedländer, David, 4–7; marriage to daughter of Daniel
Itzig, 5; Mendelssohn's heir,
46n. 5; *Miscellaneous Documents Concerning the Reform*,
103, 109; *Open Letter to Provost*

175